Put to the Test

An Educator's and Consumer's Guide to Standardized Testing

WRITTEN BY
Gerald W. Bracey

DIRECTED BY
Phillip Harris

COORDINATED BY
Alan Backler

EDITED BY
Bruce Smith

DESIGNED BY
Joyce Koeper

ILLUSTRATIONS BY
Jem Sullivan

PUBLISHED BY
Center for Professional Development & Services

Phi Delta Kappa International
408 N. Union Street
Bloomington, Indiana
47402-0789
812/339-1156

PREFACE

At the 1996 "Education Summit," the nation's governors expressed great interest in establishing standards and in creating assessments by which to evaluate their states' performance on the standards and by which to compare their states one to another. Even whole nations are rated and ranked on the basis of how well their 9- and 13-year-old students score on tests. Are these rankings fair? Important?

President Clinton keeps stating that he wants his legacy to be in the area of education. How does he propose to establish this legacy? In large part, by establishing national tests in reading and mathematics.

It is clear that tests are important to us in our daily lives. But, unfortunately, there is a great deal more you should know about the uses and abuses of testing in America. There are a great number of myths and misconceptions surrounding the ways in which tests are made and used.

It is not the case that a test is a test is a test. Tests are like automobiles: sedans, vans, and sports cars differ from one another in important ways, and so do different kinds of tests. To use tests wisely we need to know something about them. Otherwise, we get used by them.

Hence, this booklet.

TABLE OF CONTENTS

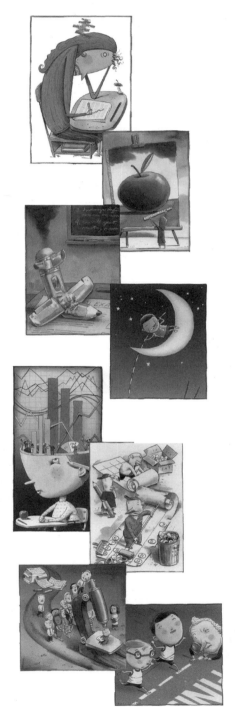

CHAPTER 1

Testing, Testing, Testing

Believe it or not, 30 years ago no one paid much attention to test scores. Few states had testing programs. There were no minimum-competency tests for high school graduation (except in Denver). Scores on the SAT were just beginning to decline, and only college applicants, high school counselors, and college admissions officers were paying any attention to SAT scores. The National Assessment of Educational Progress (NAEP, pronounced "Nape") did not exist. People had no international comparisons to show how well the U.S. stacked up against other nations on tests. No one would have dreamed of giving a "readiness" test to see if children were ready for kindergarten.

Today, tests are everywhere. Even minute changes in SAT scores make front-page news stories (at least, when the scores go down; when the scores go up, as they have for the last three years, the story gets buried). The NAEP is now routinely referred to as "the nation's report card," and it has recently introduced state-by-state comparisons in reading, mathematics, and science. Most states have at least one testing program, and many have several. School districts in South Carolina can be declared "bankrupt" and subject to state takeover if their test scores aren't up to snuff, and districts in Michigan can lose their accreditation for the same reason. Students are selected for special education and for programs for the gifted and talented largely (sometimes solely) on the basis of test scores. Teachers and administrators are given bonuses or fired because of test scores. Students are retained in grade or denied graduation because of test scores. In recent years, a great deal of excitement

> Why have tests become so important? The short answer is that people lost confidence in their schools and the people who run them.

— and perhaps even more confusion — has been generated by the concept of "authentic testing," a phrase that implies that other testing is somehow not real. At the "Education Summit" of March 1996, the nation's governors expressed enthusiasm for developing a set of high academic standards in each state, along with tests to measure whether the standards were being met and to permit the states to compare themselves to one another.

Usually, educators who hold press conferences consider themselves lucky if more than 10 reporters attend. But at the November 20, 1996, press conference on the release of the test results from the Third International Mathematics and Science Study (TIMSS), 300 people showed up. There were enough TV cameras in the room to make the affair look like Oscar night in Hollywood. In spite of the fact that the "news" was not very exciting — American kids were slightly above average in science, slightly below average in math — the story made the front-page of the *New York Times,* the *Washington Post, USA Today,* and probably most papers around the nation.

Why have tests become so important? The short answer is that people lost confidence in their schools and the people who run them.

After the end of World War II, schools were seen for the first time as integral to national defense. We were locked in weapons and space races with the Soviet Union, and schools were seen as a way to provide the large numbers of mathematicians, scientists, and engineers necessary to win. Some, like Adm. Hyman Rickover and CIA chief, Allen Dulles, contended that the schools were not up to the task. "Let us never forget," said Rickover, "that there can be no second place in a contest with Russia and that there will be no second chance if we lose." Criticism of the schools, always abundant, increased.

In October 1957, the Russians launched *Sputnik,* the first man-made satellite. To the school critics, *Sputnik* proved that they had been right all along. The critics' answer at this time was not to test children, but to provide them with new, improved curricula. Most of these curricula were developed at universities such as MIT and Stanford, and hopes for them were high because they were being created by some of the finest minds in the nation. Unfortunately, these fine minds had no experience with schools and, indeed, were trying to circumvent those who did. During this period, the phrase "teacher-proof" became common. But, by ignoring the people in the schools, the curriculum makers guaranteed that their products would fail — and they mostly did.

The schools never recovered from *Sputnik.* In a marvelous little 1989 book, *Popular Education and Its Discontents,* the distinguished education historian, Lawrence Cremin, noted that the expansion of both secondary and university education after World War II was unprecedented. But he also observed that "this expansion was accompanied by a pervasive sense of failure. The question would have to be, why?"

That is, indeed, the question, and, aside from the national defense concerns cited above, there really is no rational answer save to say that the public schools are an easy target because they are so public and because the typical reaction of school people to criticism is to work harder, not to defend themselves. In 1970, journalist Charles Silberman observed that of over a hundred studies comparing scores on tests from some time in the past to some more recent time, virtually all of them favored the more recent point in history. Yet Silberman titled his book *Crisis in the Classroom.*

For those worried about the quality of the schools, the question became, If we can't trust people in schools to tell us about how well they are functioning, what can we trust? In looking around for means by which to evaluate schools, various outsiders discovered tests.

Tests were external. Tests seemed objective. Best of all, tests in their multiple-choice formats were cheap. And once electronic scoring of answer sheets became a reality, the results could be known quickly.

Against this backdrop of increasing usage of tests came a couple of important historical events. In 1976, the College Entrance Examination Board put together a committee to study what was then a 13-consecutive-year decline in scores of the Scholastic Aptitude Test (SAT). The committee attributed a great deal of the decline to the fact that colleges were now admitting more women, more minorities, and more students with low grade-point averages. It also fingered the cultural events of the late Sixties and early Seventies as potential causes: the civil rights movement, the women's movement, the formation of a counter culture, the recreational use of drugs, urban riots, Watergate, Vietnam, Kent State, and the assassinations of Martin Luther King and Robert F. Kennedy — all of which worked together to create what the committee called "a decade of distraction."

The committee's conclusions, though, were not those of the media and thus not those of the public. The committee had asked, "What has caused the SAT score decline?" The committee had answered, "A large number of factors, acting together in complex ways." The media are seldom interested in complicated answers, though. The media saw the decline as a decline in quality of schooling. The committee's report also served to draw a great deal of attention to the SAT, and each tiny change in scores each year started appearing on the front pages of the nation's newspapers. The SAT, referred to as a "mere supplement" by its developer, now became the platinum rod for measuring schools.

Suddenly, there were tests for basic skills, for high school graduation, for teacher certification, and for accountability. The proper way of evaluating a school takes a lot of money and effort and time spent in the school. Lacking the energy or resources to conduct such evaluations, reformers relied on tests, even though the reformers usually had very little firsthand knowledge about how to build a test or how to use the results.

The SAT decline continued until 1983, and in that year a "paper *Sputnik*" was launched with the publication of *A Nation at Risk.* Fueled by inflammatory rhetoric suggesting that if an unfriendly foreign power imposed our schools on us we would consider it an act of war, *Risk* became the launching pad both for new anxieties about schools and for new efforts to reform them. Many of those reforms called for increased use of tests. As discussed in the opening paragraphs of this section, tests are now everywhere, but their increased use has not been accompanied by increased knowledge of their nature, their uses, their misuses, or their limits. Although a 1997 story in the *New York Times* stated that most experts now consider *Risk* as only very good propaganda, its impact is seen directly in the many calls for national or state standards and national or state tests.

> Unfortunately, the increased use and reporting of tests has not always been accompanied by increased understanding of how tests can or ought to be used.

People have come to accept tests without questioning their accuracy or appropriateness. If the SAT scores are falling, that must mean that school quality is declining (not necessarily so). If Japanese students score high on tests, it must mean that their schools are good (not necessarily so).

Unfortunately, the increased use and reporting of tests has not always been accompanied by increased understanding of how tests can or ought to be used. Teachers need to know what the tests can and cannot say about children. They need to be able to evaluate whether or not the decisions made about children (and themselves) on the basis of test scores are fair and appropriate. Administrators need to know about tests to determine what policy decisions about the district — and the administrators in it — are appropriate.

There is, then, a need for clear and objective information about what tests can and cannot do, about how they are constructed, and about how they are used and misused. It is my hope that this booklet will prove to be a source of such information.

A WORD ON TECHNICALITIES

Classroom tests are informally constructed assessments with none of the item-tryouts and committee review and statistics associated with commercial tests. They are ways of representing teachers' judgments about how well students are performing. Once we leave the realm of classroom assessments, though, we enter a new realm, called psychometrics, that is full of statistics and technical terms. They cannot be avoided if we are to be able to fully understand tests.

And, increasingly, people need to understand. In 1997 I was one of the expert witnesses at a court hearing to determine whether or not a particular school district could or could not use a test to retain students in grade. While a lot of the testimony presented evidence that retention in grade does not work well, period, a whole batch of other testimony turned on the fact that the test's "standard error of measurement" was too large for the school to use the test in promotion/retention decisions.

We pointed out that, given a particular "observed score," the student's "true score" could easily exceed the "cut score" needed for promotion. While we tried to talk in plain English and not in formulas, we did have to define all of the terms in quotes above in order to make our point.

As tests assume more and more visibility as means of holding students, teachers, and others accountable for school outcomes, these terms will be increasingly used in the popular culture, and, therefore, the reader needs some familiarity with them. In this booklet, these terms are discussed toward the end of the book so that they do not impede the reader who is mostly interested in types of tests and how they are used. They can be referred to as needed, or readers can peruse that section at the outset to become familiar with the terms and keep them in mind as they read the rest of the book.

A TEST ON TESTING

We end this chapter with a quiz. The answers and a short explanation for each question appear on the next page. More details can be found in the booklet that follows. The questions are all true-false. Good luck.

1. (T) (F) If a school district's high school graduates do not all read at grade level, the district is not doing its job of educating the students.

2. (T) (F) If the average total SAT score at the university you most want to go to is 1100 and your total SAT score is only 1040, you shouldn't bother to apply.

3. (T) (F) If in the Mark Twain School, Mrs. Smith's students do not score as high as Mrs. Jones' students, Mrs. Smith is not as good a teacher as Mrs. Jones.

4. (T) (F) If a school adopts a new curriculum and test scores fall, the new curriculum is shown to be inferior to the old curriculum.

5. (T) (F) The scores on a test naturally fall along a "normal"— bell-shaped — curve.

6. (T) (F) If two curricula are compared and the students using curriculum A score statistically significantly higher than the students using curriculum B, then curriculum A is the better curriculum.

7. (T) (F) A fourth-grade student reading at seventh-grade level should be promoted to the seventh grade, at least for reading instruction.

8. (T) (F) The SAT is a "common yardstick," meaning that two students with the same score from different states have the same potential for college.

9. (T) (F) If a child who scored at the 63rd percentile in reading one year falls to the 57th percentile in the next year, something is wrong. Either the child isn't trying, or the second year's teacher is not as effective.

10. (T) (F) Research indicates that IQ is 80% inherited.

THE ANSWERS

All of the statements in the quiz are false.

1. Most tests define "grade level" as the score of the average child at a given grade. For a particular school, all children could possibly be above grade level — if the school were excellent or located in an affluent neighborhood or both. But nationally half of all students are, by definition, below average — that is, below grade level.

2. If the average total SAT score is 1100, this means that half the incoming freshmen are accepted with scores below this average.[1] Your 1040 might well be acceptable. In addition, you are not in competition with all other applicants. If that were true, universities would not only be unable to field athletic teams, but they would also be unable to have fine arts or performing arts departments. Like athletes, students with these special talents often have trouble with paper-and-pencil tests. However, if your parents went to the same school or can afford to pay all of your expenses, your chances of admission are mightily improved.

3. There are many possible reasons why the classes could differ. Mrs. Smith might not emphasize material that the test covers as much as Mrs. Jones does. Mrs. Smith might also be a newer teacher; veteran teachers are often rewarded by being assigned to high-achieving classes.

4. The new curriculum might not match the test as well as the old curriculum. Tests measure highly specific aspects of a curriculum in highly specific ways. One study found that, three years after a district changed tests, the students did not score nearly as well on the old test as they did when it was routinely used.

5. Many tests will fall along a bell-shaped curve, but often such a curve is forced on the test data by the test maker through the use of "item-selection techniques" and others

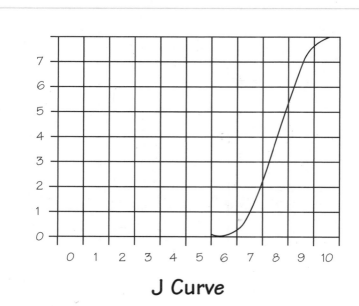

J Curve

statistical procedures. Many educators strive to make scores fall along a curve that looks like this, often called a "j" curve because it resembles the letter "j." On a bell curve, most students have learned something, a few have learned a lot, and a few have learned little. On a "j" curve, most students have learned a lot, and only a few have learned little.

6. A statistically significant difference might have no practical implications at all. Remember that a statement of statistical significance is a statement of odds: how likely it is that the difference between curriculum A and curriculum B would be seen if the two curricula were really the same. (If this seems puzzling now, not to worry; this is the most technical concept in the book and will be explained in some detail.)

7. The fourth-grade student with a seventh-grade reading level has the same score as the average seventh-grader would get when reading *fourth-grade material,* not seventh-grade material.

8. Consider two students. One comes from a well-educated, affluent family and attends an elite, private, college-preparatory high school. This student scores 600 on the SAT verbal. The other student comes from an impoverished inner-city neighborhood, attends a public school with few books, has no quiet place to study, and works to help the family make ends meet. This second student also scores 600 on the SAT verbal. Are these two students equally likely to be successful in college?

9. I don't think any published data exist to answer this question directly, but when I looked at the scores of elementary school students over a four-year period, most students varied over that period by about 25 percentile ranks. Those above the 95th percentile varied less, but only those at the 99th percentile and those below the 10th percentile tended to have really stable scores.

10. Researchers differ wildly over the relative influence on IQ of genetics and environment. What's more, the whole question might be meaningless anyway.

CHAPTER 2

Some Basic Considerations

This chapter will consider a number of fundamental issues related to standardized testing — testing and the purpose of education, the uses of tests, secrecy, factors influencing scores, and distinctions among aptitude, ability, and achievement tests.

TESTING AND THE PURPOSE OF EDUCATION

Tests in this country have historically been used to sort people: officers and enlisted men; college material and vocational school material; gifted and talented and the rest of us; bluebirds and robins. In fact, the schools themselves have sometimes been called "The Great Sorting Machine." Some people argue that sorting is a fundamental *purpose* of schools — to get people into the appropriate societal slots. Others argue that the schools should educate all children to the highest possible levels. Both positions have had prominent followers, and the debates between the two positions have been heated, to say the least.

The most obvious use of testing as a sorting device occurs in tracking, wherein some students are permitted to study more advanced topics than are other students. The early testers saw tracking as humane: to confront a child of low ability with the same curriculum as provided to a child of high ability would only frustrate and humiliate the low-ability student. This attitude exists in many places today, although its expression is muted because in the tenor of these times it is not "politically correct." And, in fact, it might also be wrong.

Even more muted is a belief among some that more resources should be allocated to abler students because it is from this group that society will get the biggest return on its investment. Few are willing to voice this belief because of its obviously elitist stance. Charles Murray, co-author of *The Bell Curve* and one of the few willing to take this stance in public, contends, "Just because it's elitist doesn't make it wrong."

For others, the purpose of education is to assist *all* children to be all that they can be. Tracking, sorting, grouping, classifying — whatever it was called — denies some students the opportunity to be other than hewers of wood and drawers of water and therefore betrays the fundamental precepts on which America was founded.

Uses of Standardized Tests

This section discusses the common uses of standardized tests, including those uses which are really not legitimate.

Monitoring. Tests are sometimes used by teachers and parents as a kind of "reality check" to see if the test results for a child accord with other indicators of achievement, such as classroom performance and report card grades. Testers like to emphasize that tests are external to the classroom and "objective," in contrast to the "subjective" judgments of teachers. A teacher's judgments are fallible, of course, but so are tests, and the teacher's "subjective" judgments are based on her observing the child over a much longer period of time. Thus the tests can be misused in this fashion if people put too much faith in the test over the other information.

Unfortunately, teachers have contributed to a growing faith in test results over grades because of the perception of "grade inflation" over the past 20 years or so. As people have come to distrust the meaning of grades, they have looked to some external instrument, and usually the only one around is some kind of test. (One wonders how many parents distrust grades because they have successfully persuaded a teacher to alter them for their children.)

Diagnosis. While there are tests designed to diagnose particular conditions that might merit

Tests in this country have historically been used to sort people: officers and enlisted men; college material and vocational school material; gifted and talented and the rest of us; bluebirds and robins.

some special education programs for a child, it is very difficult to use the typical commercial achievement test in a diagnostic fashion. There are too few items in any one skill area to give a very reliable indication at the level of the individual child. It is difficult to assess particular problems in reading comprehension, for example. In the area of arithmetic, there is more opportunity for diagnostic work because the skills are more precisely defined. It is possible to see, for instance, if a child is having difficulty with place value or with converting fractions to decimals.

Even here, though, the test is not very diagnostic and certainly not prescriptive. The best analogy might be to liken the test to a thermometer. An above normal temperature tells you that something is wrong, but, by itself, it provides no clues about what is wrong and suggests no prescription for what to do about it.

Teacher Accountability. This is one of the most seductive uses of tests because, on the surface, it seems so reasonable. Of course a teacher should be accountable for what her students know. However, there are a variety of problems with using tests for teacher accountability. In the first place, one teacher might emphasize what is on the test while another prefers to teach other subject matter and can provide good justifications for what she is offering. Not everything can be taught, and two teachers may well differ on how to teach the same material. One could elect to teach science through physics, another through ecology. One could elect to present science as a series of disciplines, another could emphasize science as a process and focus on the scientific method that cuts across disciplines. Of course, if the tests *are* used for accountability, teachers *will* come to emphasize what is on them.[*]

There are other problems with tests and teacher accountability. The process collides with the common system of assigning teachers to classrooms. Logically, one might think that the best teachers would be assigned the toughest classes. In many places, the reverse holds: the perception of good teaching is rewarded by assignments to high-achieving classes. High test scores for one teacher

---

[*] Perhaps the most vivid example of this practice occurred in Prince George's County, Maryland, in the 1980s. Superintendent John Murphy arrived, as most new superintendents do, announcing a number of goals for the district. One was get test scores up overall and to close the gap between the scores of black students and white students. Murphy established one room in the administration building as his "applied anxiety room," a room in which the test score trends for all school buildings were charted on the walls. As the years passed, test scores did rise. And the ethnic gap, while it did not vanish, narrowed substantially. Black students, who constitute about 65% of the children in the Prince George's County system, were scoring comfortably above the national norm.

But there were informal reports that instruction in some Prince George's County schools looked a lot like taking a test. Children would go to the blackboard and select one of four or five answers to a problem or question. Several organizations requested permission to conduct external evaluations of the programs. Murphy refused. The state of Maryland used this test for more years than it should have, but it finally adopted a new test. Often when a new test is brought into a state, scores go down. New item formats, new content, etc. all operate to lower scores a bit. The year the new test was adopted, scores went down all over Maryland. The drop was more noticeable than usual, probably because the state had used the old test so long. But in Prince George's County the scores did not just fall, they plummeted: some scores for black students fell as low as the 18th percentile. Fortunately for Murphy, he had accepted a job in another state.

might reflect good teaching, but they might also reflect the ability level of the students.

Children do not arrive in a teacher's classroom as blank slates. They come with previous levels of achievement. These levels of achievement are greatly dependent on what happens and has happened outside of school. From birth to age 18, an American child is in school 9% of his or her life. The external environment affects test scores a great deal.

A rational approach to the use of tests as accountability devices for teachers might be to test the children in the fall and use these test scores and a variety of demographic variables to predict test scores at the end of the year. The end-of-year scores could then be matched against the predictions. It would be necessary, of course, to ensure that the test actually reflected what had been — or should have been — taught during the year. This kind of match of predicted against actual scores, if reasonable, is complicated and expensive, and therefore virtually no one does it.[**] Something like it has been done for a number of years in Tennessee with interesting outcomes. No predictions are involved, but 11 years of research have generated pretty consistent results: teachers who produce large gains one year are likely to do so the next. Teachers who produce little or no gain one year are unlikely to improve the next.

[**] There is a general problem with accountability that goes beyond testing in schools. People strive to make themselves look good. Period. When organizations started rating airlines on the percentage of on-time arrivals, the times to fly from one place to another got longer. Airlines built a lot of fudge time into their schedules. I travel a lot, and it is often the case that we arrive early.

People should be wary about attempts to use tests to make schools or districts look good. One recent example of this kind of misuse involves giving a test to students in the fall and again in the spring but scoring the test both times with spring norms. The spring norms reflect growth from fall to spring. The students might not look so good in the fall, but the school will be able to show a lot of growth. This would be true even if the children didn't learn much during the year.

Principal/Superintendent/Board Accountability.
There are states, such as Michigan and North Carolina, where the consequences of low test scores are visited not upon the teachers but upon one or more of the school's or district's administrators. These programs are too new to know what actual impact they will have. In North Carolina, if a school is declared low achieving, it receives assistance from the state, and its principal is put on probation. In one instance where this happened in 1997, the district sued the state.

All the considerations mentioned under teacher accountability apply here as well. There are various ways of predicting test score outcomes that take into account the demographic conditions of a school. One method is to compare a particular school to other schools with similar demographics. This method was used in California for some years. Some schools were unhappy about what the state considered "comparable schools," but, since there were no real sanctions attached, the issue was not pressed.

North Carolina uses the other major technique, using the school's demographics to set growth targets and then using test scores to see if the targets have been achieved. As noted, the programs are in their infancy, and it is too soon to evaluate them.

Student Accountability: Promotion, Retention, and Graduation Decisions. There appears to be a growing trend in this country to use tests for decisions about promotion and retention and about eligibility for graduation.

About retention in grade, this much can be said: it doesn't work. Study after study has found the consequences to be negative. One study ranked 49 educational innovations in terms of their impact on achievement. Retention in grade ranked 49th. It was among the few innovations that actually produced *negative* results[*]

When tests are taken more than once, the chances of our making a bad decision about a child are reduced. If a child gets, say, three shots at a test, it is far less likely that three low scores are the result of "measurement error" (discussed in the section

on technical issues) than if the test had been taken only once.

Still, no matter how often we administer a test, its scores should never be used alone for making important decisions about students. Indeed, the American Educational Research Association, the American Psychological Association, and the National Council for Measurement in Education have published standards for test development and use which consider the use of test scores alone for such decisions as grave ethical violations. In the section on the SAT, its principal developer, Carl Campbell Brigham, is quoted as regarding it "as merely a supplemental record" to the rest of the high school record. This is a wise approach toward all test use.

Tests currently used for graduation eligibility are for the most part not commercial achievement tests, but tests constructed ostensibly around state curricula. Students typically get six or more attempts at them before graduation time so the likelihood of a student not passing despite having an achievement level well above what the test reports is quite small. Whether or not the test is testing what high school students should know is another question, one that needs to be evaluated in each instance.

---

[*] Why do people continue to believe that retention works? Largely because they are not in a position to conduct a controlled experiment. Most teachers and parents are in a position only to watch the retained child in his second year in a grade. Most children do better the second time around, but not a whole lot better. Few bloom into high achievers. Parents and teachers observing a child struggling in the same grade a second year then assume that the child's difficulties would have been that much worse if the child had been promoted.

There have been occasions when some low-achieving children were retained and others with the same low achievement were promoted. In the next year the promoted children did as well as or better than their retained peers.

Selection Decisions. As noted at the beginning of this chapter, tests were designed to make discriminations among people in order to provide some people one set of educational experiences (officer candidate school, college entry, a more challenging curriculum, etc.) and other people different educational experiences. The hope has always been to match the experiences to people's needs and abilities, but it has not always worked out that way.

In selection for college, admissions officers have a great deal of information about students, often going beyond SAT (or ACT) scores, grades, and rank in class. Many colleges now ask for essays and/or personal interviews with alumni in the field, and students themselves sometimes send in videotapes.

Currently, almost half the students who start college don't finish. This was true when I matriculated in 1958, but society's attitude about it is different now. I recall the dean of men at the public college I attended proudly announcing at the first fall convocation that 50% of us would not make it. He saw the 50% figure as upholding the college's standards. Currently, it is viewed with alarm as a "dropout rate." Whichever way we see it, it indicates that the admissions process, tests and all, is not highly accurate.

Actually, as many observers have pointed out, there is little evidence that most colleges are "selecting" students. From 1977 to 1994, the number of high school graduates declined each year as the baby boom bottomed out. Yet college enrollments rose by over 4,000,000 during the same period. Instead of cutting faculty, staff, and programs as the number of high school graduates declined, many colleges shifted from selecting students to recruiting them. I recall my two children, good but not exceptional students in high school, receiving lots of glossy, full color brochures touting the virtues of various colleges. It is still true that only about one applicant in seven gets admitted to schools like Amherst, Brown, and Harvard, but these elite schools are few in number.

In selecting students for gifted and talented programs or other enrichment programs, tests often play a dominant role — sometimes the only role. Occasionally, a group-administered IQ test is used as the criterion, more often a commercial achievement test. Typically, a certain percentile is used as a cut score. Some room is left for teacher nomination and parental pressure as well. In districts with diverse populations, the administration sometimes resorts to a percentage of top scores rather than a percentile. The top, say, 5% of test scorers are selected into the program, allowing all schools to have similar-sized programs. Naturally, the schools in the more affluent parts of the district protest because some students excluded in these schools would qualify in a less affluent school.

Selection into special education programs is not usually quite so test dependent. This is good because the tests used for diagnosis of special needs, though they are specialized tests, often do not have as high reliability as the typical achievement tests. Decisions for special education selection are made, or at least should be made, in a group consultation involving teachers, the parents, and the special education specialists of the district.

SECRECY

If you are surprised to see a segment on secrecy ("test security" it's usually called) because you don't think it's an issue, then your next reaction should be fear because you have been seduced into accepting as natural a most unusual, even pathological situation. In *Assessing Student Performance*, Grant Wiggins captured the setting and our all too usual casual reaction to it well:

> It is so common that we barely give it a second thought: the tests that we and others design to evaluate the success of student learning invariably depend upon secrecy. Secrecy as to the questions that will be asked. Secrecy as to how the questions will be chosen. Secrecy as to how the results will be scored. Sometimes secrecy as to when we will be tested. Secrecy as to what the scores mean. Secrecy as to how the results will be used. What a paradoxical affair!

Our aim is to educate, to prepare, to enlighten, yet our habits of testing are built upon procedures that continually keep students in the dark — procedures with roots in premodern traditions of legal proceedings and religious inquisitions.[2]

Actually, the situation is worse than that because Wiggins has only the students in mind. But most of the time the teachers don't know what is going on either. In many school testing programs, the tests are kept away from teachers until the very last minute.

Wiggins notes that the secrecy aspect of testing helps produce people who are both docile (they put up with it) and leery. The point is made also by anthropologist F. Allan Hanson in his book *Testing Testing: Social Consequences of the Examined Life,* "Whether the results are positive or negative is irrelevant. The point is that testing opens the self to scrutiny and investigation in ways that the self is powerless to control. So far as the areas of knowledge covered by the test are concerned, this transforms the person from autonomous subject to passive object."[3]

Both Wiggins and Hanson observe that testing increases the power of the tester over the tested and that the aspect of secrecy enhances this power differential. Wiggins likens the situation to the story of the Emperor's new clothes. Secrecy allows test makers to insist that only people with their special skills can produce tests. The situation is not likely to improve soon.

FACTORS INFLUENCING TEST SCORES

Discussions about tests in the media often make it seem like only what happens in school has any impact on test scores. This is hardly true. After all, a child only spends 9% of his or her life from birth to age 18 in school. We should keep in mind the following factors in thinking about test scores.

Family Income. If you look at the College Board's *Profiles of College-Bound Seniors,* which comes out each fall with the release of SAT scores, you will see one table showing SAT scores by income level. There is a very clear progression: the higher the income, the higher the SAT score.

Educational Level of Parents. In many studies, the parents' educational level is the single biggest factor contributing to the test scores of children. Incidentally, the educational level of Asian Americans is much higher than that of the country as a whole.

Poverty. One study examined scores in high- and low-poverty schools. High-poverty schools were defined as those in which at least 76% of the students were eligible for free or reduced price lunches. Low-poverty schools had zero to 20% eligibility rates. The researchers first divided the students into groups depending on the kinds of letter grades they took home on report cards. Then they looked to see how these groups performed on standardized tests of reading and math. Students in low-poverty schools who got A's scored about as you would expect, averaging the 81st percentile in reading and the 87th in math. Students in high-poverty schools who got A's scored higher than students who got lower grades, but in neither case did the average score reach even the 40th percentile.

Motivation. Motivation can have an enormous impact on scores. I tell a specific story about this on page 48.

Personal Hygiene. I use this term to cover things like getting a good night's sleep before the day of testing and eating well on the day of testing. Hungry children do not score as high as well-fed children.

Cultural Factors. This is another global category to cover a number of influences. In the Third International Mathematics and Science Study (TIMSS), most of the 41 countries participating, especially western countries, had eighth-grade test scores that were very similar to one another. Five or six developing nations scored at the bottom, and four Asian nations — Singapore, Japan, Korea, and Hong Kong scored high. (Taiwan did not take part; it would probably have been another high scorer.) In between were about 30 nations with few differences. In the high-scoring nations it is not unusual for students to go to school after school or to go to a private tutor. They also go to school on weekends.

Here's a typical report from Japan:

> Akiko Tsutui, a 10-year-old fifth-grader, gets out of school at 3:30 p.m. and goes straight home to have a snack and do her homework. Three afternoons a week she leaves again at 4:45 for a *juku* (cram school for tests) session that lasts from 5:10 to 10:00. For almost the entire class, Akiko will listen to tutors explain how to answer test questions and will practice taking them herself. [4]

And this from Korea:

> It was 11 p.m. and fourth-grader Moon Sae Bom was solving math problems and double-checking her social studies maps. For the past two hours, her mother had sat beside her, checking her answers, making sure the 10-year-old didn't fall asleep.
>
> Across this academically hyperachieving county, students file out of public and private high schools not at 3 p.m. but at 10 p.m. Every weeknight they study in their classrooms from dinner until late into the evening. [5]

The story, from a reporter based in Tokyo, contends that many South Koreans now spend 20% to 30% of their incomes on private tutors. It also states that "today's South Korean students make the famously intense Japanese students look easygoing."

Students in these countries also have additional motivations. In Japan, for example, it is critically important for the future that children get into the "right" high school and even more important later to get into the "right" college. In the January 1998 issue of *Principal*, Kazuo Ishizaka, president of the Japanese Council on Global Education, writes, "Because Japanese society judges people on the basis of the schools they attended rather than their ability and skills, Japanese parents try to send their children to the best schools." [6]

When I lived in Hong Kong, the exams given at the end of eighth grade were even more life-determining because there was room in high schools for only 25% of the eighth-grade students. Suicide hotlines were set up to handle calls from those most distraught by their failure to obtain a place in a high school.

Under such conditions, it is not surprising to find students in these countries outscoring European and American students. The American vision of high school life includes malls, dating, cars, jobs, and extracurricular activities at school. American kids are expected to crank it up, brainwise, in college. And they do. In contrast, Japanese students work extremely hard in high school, but stories abound of how they go into intellectual hibernation once they reach college. Their life has been pretty much determined by getting into an institution of higher education. They might very well already know what company they will work for when they graduate. [*]

---

[*] We should probably observe in passing that while Americans have been wondering how to get students' test scores up in international comparisons, high Asian education officials have been visiting America to see how they can make their students more like ours. A June 9, 1997, editorial in *The Daily Yomiuri* declared that the Japanese school system was "obsolete and useless for the development of society." According to the editorial, the system doesn't develop artistic or cultural sensibility, doesn't promote an international perspective or social awareness, and "is ineffective in developing students' ability to think for themselves." In a 1997 visit to the United States, the Minister of Education of Singapore, the highest-scoring nation in TIMSS, expressed disdain that the only thing his students could do was answer test questions.

APTITUDE, ABILITY, AND ACHIEVEMENT TESTS

Few notions in testing have caused more mischief than the distinctions between aptitude, ability, and achievement tests. Conceptually, the three are indistinguishable. Ability and aptitude tests do not measure something qualitatively different from what achievement tests measure.

The trouble begins when people assume, as they all too often do, that an aptitude or ability test measures "potential." Given a measure of potential, we can then label children as "where they ought to be," "underachievers," or "overachievers," according to whether their performance in school compares to their performance on the test. We could with just as much logic label a child an "overtester" or "undertester."

That there is no conceptual distinction between ability tests and achievement tests has been known for many years, but it is something that just doesn't enter into the everyday discussion of tests. When the National Research Council, part of the National Academy of Sciences, conducted an extensive study of ability testing, it found citations as early as 1927 declaring that the two "types" of tests were fundamentally the same. The Council concluded:

> The line of demarcation between aptitude and achievement tests is not as clear-cut as popularly believed. The major difference has been well stated by Anne Anastasi: "Today the difference between these two types of tests is chiefly one of degree of specificity of content and extent to which the test presupposes a designated course of instruction."[7]

The Council's citation from Anastasi, an eminent psychometrician, comes from the 1976 edition of her textbook on testing. More recently, Anastasi affirmed her position.

> We should especially guard against the naive assumption that achievement tests measure the effects of learning while aptitude tests measure

"innate capacity" independent of learning. This misconception was fairly prevalent in the early days of psychological testing but has been largely corrected in the subsequent clarification of psychological concepts. It should be obvious that all psychological tests measure the individual's current behavior, which inevitably reflects the influence of prior learning.[8]

The point is so important, and the misconception so ingrained in our culture that I risk the reader's attention with one more citation, this one from perhaps the most eminent psychometrician alive today, Lee Cronbach:

> An aptitude test is one intended to predict success in some occupation or training course — these are tests of engineering aptitude, musical aptitude, aptitude for algebra, and so on. These tests are not distinct in form [from achievement tests]. The achievement/aptitude contrast is one of point of view, more than test content. Any test is an achievement test inasmuch as it is a report on development and learning to date; and it is an aptitude test in as much as it says something about the future.[9]

An achievement test looks back in time; an ability or aptitude test looks forward. Thus, in fact, any test can be used for both purposes. We typically use the SAT to predict college success, and we use tests such as the Stanford Achievement Tests to summarize accomplishment in high school. But there is no reason why we couldn't use the Stanford to predict college success. Such prediction is merely a statistical process, the calculation of a correlation coefficient (discussed in the section on technicalities). We take the scores from our test — SAT or Stanford or any other test — and correlate those scores with the freshmen grade-point averages of those we tested.

We could use high school grade-point averages to predict success in college — and they actually work better than the SAT at most universities. We could even use height or weight to predict college success, though the predictions might not be very useful. All we need to predict first-year college success are two variables: college freshman grade-point averages and any number that varies — height, weight, SAT scores, finger length, etc. Remember, any two variables can be correlated. Whether or not the correlation is meaningful is another question. Predicting college grades from the SAT merely means correlating these two variables, a simple statistical procedure.

The real difference between ability and aptitude tests on the one hand and achievement tests on the other is that we have a better idea of how a student came to do well or not so well on an achievement test. Even if an achievement test doesn't wholly reflect the curriculum — e.g., a phonics-based reading test given to a whole-language class — it still reflects to some extent what is being learned in school, reading. Ability tests often don't. For instance, the Cognitive

Abilities Test (CogAT) includes a "nonverbal" section that requires students, among other things, to look at a series of geometrical forms and choose from a selection of forms presented the one that would be next in the series. Some kids are really good at this, and some are awful. But it is unlikely that any of them received instruction in "geometric form prediction" from their teachers.*

To repeat: in a single sitting, with a test given only once, you cannot measure potential. You can measure only what the student knows and can do at the time you test him. You can use that measure to look either forward or backward in time.

It is possible that a more meaningful index of ability could be obtained from multiple measures. If we tested a student in the fall and again in the spring and measured how much better she did in the spring than in the fall, we might use this difference as a measure of ability in terms of rate of learning, though it's still not a measure of "potential." Although this idea is plausible, no one has systematically tried to develop this notion of ability. Few people have even dabbled at it.

It is unlikely that we will stop distinguishing between ability and achievement in schools or in everyday discourse any time soon. The idea that there is such a distinction is deeply embedded in our culture and in our everyday language. In the sports world, for instance, it is common to hear commentators say that a certain athlete "has the most raw ability" of anyone on the team or that an athlete "never developed his ability fully." Similar statements are just as common in the academic realm. We just don't hear them on prime-time TV.

---

* By the way, the CogAT has two other sections, verbal and quantitative. Kids who do well on the nonverbal section and poorly on the verbal and quantitative have a terrible time coping with school — because school is all about numbers and words. Kids who have this pattern of skills are often good at art, videogames, and perceptually oriented skills like chess.

CHAPTER 3

Standardized Tests

Most of the tests that people take or are likely to read about in the newspapers are referred to as "standardized tests." The SAT is probably the best known of such tests. But anyone who has gone through the public schools is likely to have encountered the Iowa Tests of Basic Skills, Iowa Tests of Educational Development, Tests of Achievement and Proficiency, the Stanford Achievement Tests, the Comprehensive Tests of Basic Skills, or the Metropolitan Achievement Tests, all commercial standardized tests used in grades K-12.

What is standardized about standardized tests? The short answer is, almost everything. The format of all the questions for all students is the same — standardized. This format is usually, but not always, the multiple-choice format. All the questions for all students are the same — standardized. (Well into the 20th century, examinations were often oral, with each student getting different questions.) The instructions to all students are the same — standardized. The time permitted for all students to complete the test is the same — standardized. Standardized tests are often contrasted with "teacher made" tests, but even these share many of the standardized characteristics listed above.

Standardized tests are most often administered to groups of students, but some, such as IQ tests, can be given to individuals. In such cases, those who administer the tests have themselves been highly "standardized." That is, while they have some flexibility in the sequencing of questions and in applying the criteria for a correct answer, they must undergo extensive training to become standardized in the way the tests are given and scored. A child should not get an IQ of 100 from one test administrator and 130 from another.

About the only thing in the arena of standardized testing that is not standardized is the test-taker. This lack of standardization among test-takers is a fact most often overlooked by test-makers and test users — except in the case of very young children where the lack of standardization is so obvious it cannot be ignored. There have been a few studies of test-taking styles and a large number of studies of text-anxious people. But for the most part these studies are ignored in districtwide or statewide testing and sometimes even in classroom testing.[*]

HOW STANDARDIZED TESTS ARE CONSTRUCTED

The methods used to construct standardized tests are themselves highly standardized, especially the methods for constructing the most commonly used tests: commercially published achievement tests used by schools. To construct these tests, test publishers cull the most common textbooks and curriculum materials and try to develop questions that reflect the content of these materials. The questions are rated by curriculum specialists for what is termed "content validity," which is simply a rating by the experts as to whether or not they think the test actually measures what it claims to.

The questions are then tried out on groups of people — standardized — to see if the questions "behave properly." Proper behavior in a test question is defined by means of statistical procedures.

We can see here one potential problem deriving from the way tests are constructed by test publishers, most of which are subsidiaries of large publishing conglomerates: the process of construction can limit educational innovation. A test publisher naturally wants to sell a test to the widest possible market in order to obtain the largest possible profit. To have such an appeal, tests have to be oriented towards that which is common among schools, not that which is unique. This can inhibit educators from trying innovations that might depart from the common denominator of material that the test covers. If schools are evaluated on the basis of test scores, education reformers will be loath to make innovations that might not be reflected in these scores.

The Key School in Indianapolis is one of the rare examples of the way an innovation can be introduced in spite of the fact that it is likely to have little or no effect on test scores. The teachers who founded the Key School, a part of the Indianapolis Public Schools, were intrigued by the theory of multiple intelligences developed by psychologist Howard Gardner of Harvard University. Gardner's theory outlines evidence for seven intelligences: linguistic, logico-mathematical, spatial, musical, bodily-kinesthetic, intrapersonal, and interpersonal. Gardner has chastised traditional schools for emphasizing only linguistic and logico-mathematical intelligences. The founders of the Key school based it on developing all seven. Thus all children learn to play a musical instrument and receive daily lessons in art. Movement is emphasized during physical education. Visitors to the Key School come away in awe. It is obvious that the kids love being there (the Key School began as a pre-kindergarten through grade 6 school; it expanded to the middle grades and high school grades in large part because its early graduates pleaded for such a school for their upper grades).

---

[*] The lack of work in this area could be an important omission. A recent study, for example, found that different students have different, but consistent, test-taking tempos when the time allowed to finish the test is not a factor. Even when there is enough time for all people to finish the test, some people will work faster than others, and this is a fairly consistent personality trait. One would expect that, when people with different tempos are put in settings where time *is* a factor — as in most test-taking situations — some people's performance will be badly disrupted.

Now many people would hold that it's a good thing to learn about art or to play a musical instrument or to speak, read, and write a foreign language. But acquiring these skills will do nothing to improve students' performance on, say, the Iowa Tests of Basic Skills (ITBS). The vocabularies of art and music are too specialized to be a part of the reading or vocabulary sections of the ITBS. Specialized words in the lower grades do not lend themselves to the kind of items that have the statistical properties test-makers are looking for (more about just what they're looking for later). Similarly, learning Spanish, the language chosen at the Key School, might one day help a student to see the Latin root of an otherwise mysterious word on the SAT, but it will not do anything for the ITBS.

A principle emerges from the above: *tests should be used to evaluate schools (or anything else) only when it is clear that the test reflects what is being taught.* A second principle also emerges: *those who make school reforms should seek instruments that might reasonably be expected to be sensitive to the effects of the changes.* If it looks like the reform ought to push test scores upward, then a test is a reasonable device to use to look for the reform's impact. But if the changes don't seem to have much relationship to test scores, then other instruments need to be sought, or tests sensitive to the reforms need to be developed.

After the Russians launched *Sputnik* in 1957, a number of people felt that the Russians were ahead in the space race because they had better curricula and tougher schools. Many projects emerged to develop new ways of teaching mathematics, physics, biology, and so on. Naturally, the question arose, Are these new curricula any better than the old ones? When students using various curricula were tested, the answer that emerged was: it depends. What it depended on was the match of the test to the curriculum. The old curricula looked good if the students took a test matched to them; the new curricula looked good if the test reflected what they attempted to teach.

> What is standardized about standardized tests? The short answer is, almost everything.

NORM-REFERENCED TESTS

A norm-referenced test (NRT) is a standardized test with norms. And the norm is a rank, the 50th percentile. It is the rank assigned to the "median" score, and the median is one kind of average.[*] It is the median score of some group. For nationally used tests, the most common norm is a national norm constructed by testing children all over the country. There are usually norms for urban and suburban schools and, for some tests,

---

[*] Some readers might have noticed that in some places on previous pages, I have referred to ranks as "scores." Technically, that is incorrect. A rank is a rank. Different scores are at different ranks, but the scores are not the ranks. Calling ranks scores is common in both writing and talking about tests because it is awkward to be absolutely correct. This confusion becomes important only when we forget that ranks alone actually obscure performance. International comparisons are often reported in ranks only. Tongues cluck over low-ranking countries. What this kind of reporting hides is that *scores* of most of the countries are very close. For instance, in one recent study of science in 41 nations, the United States ranked 19th, and *U. S. News & World Report* declared that this put us on a par with Bulgaria and Iceland. Bulgarian students got only 4% more correct answers the American kids, but this vaulted them all the way to 5th place. Icelandic students got 6% fewer items correct than American students, and this dropped them all the way to 30th place.

We can note here that test-makers and statisticians use three kinds of "average": mean, median, and mode. (See Chapter Seven: Getting Technical.)

private schools. In the case of the national norm, it is also the score that test-makers call "at grade level." By definition, then, half of all test-takers score at or above the 50th percentile, and half score below it. Half score above grade level and half score below it.

This property of norm-referenced tests bothers some people because, by definition, half of all test-takers will always be "below average." A system that labels half of our children as below average disturbs some people. It sometimes also leads to confusion — some people, politicians usually, can be heard decrying the fact that half of the students scored below average. The cries happen more frequently when the phrase "grade level" is used because, it would seem intuitively obvious that everyone in, say, the seventh grade, should be at or above grade level. People who utter such cries don't realize that this outcome was guaranteed in advance by the way the test was constructed.

A norm-referenced test gives scores in relation to the norm, the 50th percentile, hence its name. If one of your students receives a report that says he scored at the 75th percentile, you know that he scored better than 75% of the students in the nation who took the test and that 25% of the students scored better than he did. You do not know from a percentile whether your student is doing well or poorly or average in any absolute sense.

Establishing the Norm. To determine the norm, test publishers first try out their questions on students and choose the questions that behave properly. By and large, this means choosing questions that 50%

of the students miss. Some questions will be easier, and some will be harder. But rarely do tests include questions that 90% of the students get right or that 90% get wrong.

The choice of items that 50% of the students fail is an artifact of the history of testing in this country. If you want to make differential predictions, you have to arrange it so different people get different scores. If you choose items that everyone misses or everyone gets right, then everyone gets the same score, and you can't make differential predictions. It turns out that, if you choose items that, on average, 50% of the test-takers get right and 50% get wrong, you end up with a test that distributes scores in a normal, bell-shaped curve and maximizes the dispersion of the scores.

Test developers will also reject items that people with low total scores get right or that people with high total scores get wrong. They reason that there must be something peculiar about an individual item that the high-scorers have trouble with or that the low-scorers find a snap. Maybe there's something peculiar about one of the distracters (the testing industry's name for the wrong answers presented in multiple-choice questions) that's causing the high-scorers to make a mistake. Who knows? In any case, the item is dumped.

The very presence of "distracters" bothers a number of test critics. The test publishers must trick some students into choosing a wrong answer. If they cannot do that, then the item will not "behave" properly. That is, it will not be missed by half of the students. Leaving aside whether trying to trick students into making mistakes is an appropriate activity for educators, let us note that this procedure can be a barrier to good test construction under some circumstances. For instance, when I was a teaching assistant for introductory psychology at Stanford University in the 1960s, the administration wanted me to grade "on the curve," allowing 15% A's, 35% B's, 35% C's, and 15% D's and F's. This distribution approximates a normal or bell-shaped curve. Now, at that time the average total SAT score of entering freshmen at Stanford was about 1225, and 22% of them had never seen anything lower than an A on their report cards — and this was in the days before people started worrying about "grade inflation." Yet, at the directive of the university administration, 50% of these bright young people were supposed to be handed C's, D's, and F's.

The students knew this, of course, and they studied hard to be in the upper half of the distribution. This made it even more difficult to assign grades in line with the administration's wishes. If I asked questions about the important material in the chapter, everyone would get the questions right, and I would not have any differentiated scores to use as a basis for grading. It was very difficult to construct tests that would produce differential scores without resorting to asking improbably subtle questions or resorting to asking questions about material found in some obscure footnote at the end of the chapter.

The discussion in the previous paragraphs reveals something important about tests: much of what determines whether a question will be on a test has nothing to do with the content of the test. Whether a question gets on a test has to do with technical, statistical concerns about how the item "behaves."

Once the test publisher has a set of well-behaved items, the company conducts what is called a national norming study. That is, it administers the test to a large group of children, maybe as many as 200,000 in all grades. These children have been selected so that they are representative of the nation. That is, the group has the same mix of black, white, Hispanic, Asian, Native American, rich, middle class, poor, urban, suburban, and rural as the nation as a whole. The median score of this group, the 50th percentile, is then called the "national norm." By definition, half of the students will be below average.

What if a community has high percentile ranks? It could mean that all the kids are smart or that their school system is good or both. It's also possible that they're just rich. Wealthy communities in this country spend more on their schools, and families in such communities can provide enrichment at home that is unavailable to people in poorer communities. Some districts that are not average in wealth thus complain that comparing themselves to the national norm is not meaningful. To assist these communities, test publishers develop various kinds of "local norms."

For example, a suburb can compare itself to other suburbs if it so chooses. It seldom does so because the rank of the suburb in comparison to similarly advantaged communities will not look as good as a comparison to the nation as a whole. On the other hand, an impoverished city neighborhood will look better when compared to impoverished neighborhoods in other cities than to the nation as a whole.

And that illustrates a problem with "local norms" in education: they can obscure real problems. An inner-city school that adjusts its test reports to take account of local norms can say, "We're doing as well as expected, and we'd be doing just as well as the rest of the country if we didn't have all these poor kids in our buildings." But that school *does* have all those poor kids in its buildings, and children who live in poverty are at risk of just about any catastrophe you can name and require special efforts in their schooling.

Domains. We speak of tests of reading, mathematics, history, and so forth as if they were generic tests of these subjects. But they are not. They are short tests of specific skills.

Test publishers admit that their tests can't cover everything. How could they? They're only 25 to 40 items long. The publishers will contend that their tests sample a larger "domain." This theory is represented by the left circle in Figure 1. The big circle represents a domain such as mathematics. The little circles represent what the items on the test are supposed to do: they sample a representative part of the domain. This is in contrast to the right circle in Figure 1. There, the items sample only a small part of the overall domain. The theory of domain sampling is largely nonsense because no one has ever specified what a curriculum "domain" is. All the tests really do is ask specific questions in specific ways.

Multiple-Choice Format. The multiple-choice format is a peculiar way of measuring something. This can be seen most readily in connection with writing. For a number of years, when multiple-choice tests were virtually the only form used, "writing" achievement was assessed in terms of what might be more accurately called editing skill. For instance, students would look at a sentence and decide what was wrong with it by choosing one of the four or five "corrections" provided. Or the test might show a short paragraph with four or five parts of it underlined, and the student's task was to decide which underlined section contained an error (or if none of them did). Since they were being evaluated on their students' performance on tests of this type of editing skill, teachers naturally taught this type of editing skill. As a consequence, children did not learn how to write. When educators later came to their senses and realized that writing can only be taught and assessed by having kids write, children's writing improved immensely.

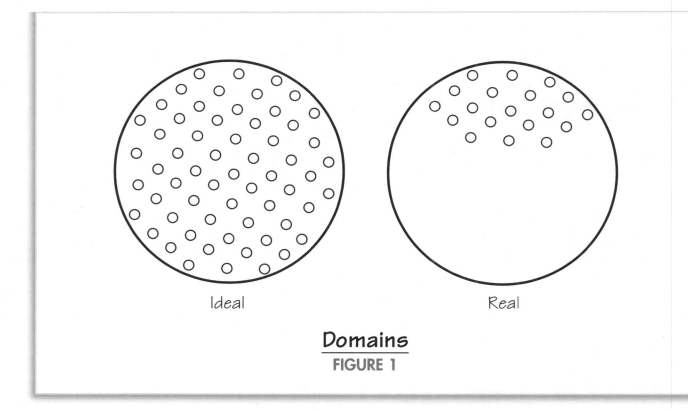

Ideal   Real

Domains
FIGURE 1

There is another aspect of multiple-choice tests that merits comment here, and it was captured wonderfully by one T. C. Batty in a 1959 letter to the *Times* of London:

> Sir,
>
> Among the "odd one out" type of questions which my son had to answer for a school entrance examination was, "Which is the odd one out among cricket, football, billiards, and hockey?"
>
> I say billiards because it is the only one played indoors. A colleague says football because it is the only one in which the ball is not struck with an implement. A neighbor says cricket because in all the other games the object is to put the ball into a net; and my son, with the confidence of nine summers, plumps for hockey "because it is the only one that is a girls' game." Could any of your readers put me out of my misery by stating what is the correct answer, and further enlighten me by explaining how questions of this sort prove anything, **especially when the scholar has merely to underline the odd one out without giving a reason?**
>
> Perhaps there is a remarkable subtlety behind all this. Is the question designed to test what a child of 9 may or may not know about billiards — proficiency at which may still be regarded as the sign of a misspent youth?
>
> Yours faithfully,
> T. C. Batty

There is not, unfortunately, any kind of "remarkable subtlety" behind such a question. Readers did not put Batty out of his misery, although they did write many letters offering still more reasons why one particular game was the odd one out. It was doubtless great fun for *Times* readers, though we might well wonder how much fun the experience was for Batty's son and his classmates. They were, after all, being evaluated, at age 9, to determine if they qualified for admission to elite schools.

I have put in bold the part of the letter that reveals an unavoidable problem with multiple-choice tests: you have no idea why students might have picked a particular answer. Did they guess? Did they recall it by rote? Did they reason their way to a right answer? Did they reason their way to a wrong answer? Young children especially can often give quite plausible reasons for choosing a wrong answer — if asked. Unfortunately, in the usual testing situation, no one asks them.

What You Test Is What You Get. One final condition of testing that deserves comment here is the Law of WYTIWYG (pronounced, wittywig): What You Test Is What You Get. There are two aspects of this law. The first and most obvious is that teachers will spend more time on the topics covered by a test than they will on topics not covered by the test, particularly if test scores are emphasized by the school staff, the school board, the media, or local industry. Thus it is very important to use tests that reflect instructional priorities and that do not in and of themselves cause the curriculum to become narrowed by teaching to the test. Teaching to most school tests is a problem because it constitutes "cheating."

But that is not the real problem. A high school football coach teaches to the test all week long, and we don't call it cheating. Indeed, we would think him crazy if he did anything else. But in this instance, the "test" is a real-life experience to get ready for. Many achievement tests, though, are in no way "real life" experiences. A teacher can teach to a test, but it comes at the expense of not teaching other parts of the curriculum. In addition, real life does not come to us in a multiple-choice format. That is the real problem of teaching to most tests, and that is one reason there has been such an increased interest over the past decade in "performance tests" — tests that measure actual performance rather than tests where students are provided the answers in multiple-choice format.

There is, however, a second and more subtle aspect of testing related to the Law of WYTIWYG: how you test determines, in part, what you see. When you measure people by means of a multiple-choice test, some people will do well, and others won't. When you measure people by means of a performance assessment, some people will do well, and others won't. But they won't be all the same people. In educational testing, how you measure something determines, in part, what you see. In addition, in the best of all testing worlds, people are indeed altered by the measurement: the best testing informs as well as assesses. Athletes often return from their "tests," saying "I learned something out there today." Students seldom walk away from a testing situation with the same sense of accomplishment.

CRITERION-REFERENCED TESTS

How a person stands relative to the norm or to other people — a normative score — is not the only possible kind of score. However, normative scores are overwhelmingly the easiest to obtain and, as a consequence, are the most common. It is possible, however, to score performance in relation to a clearly specified set of behaviors, and in the early 1960s, this fact led to the development of another type of standard test referred to as criterion referenced tests (CRTs). Most of these tests were not really criterion referenced, but that gets us ahead of our story.

What is a "clearly specified set of behaviors?" Such behaviors are hard to specify for the topics taught in school. So most examples of clearly specified behaviors were taken from other areas. The inventor of the phrase, "criterion-referenced testing," Robert Glaser of the University of Pittsburgh, said that we could imagine achievement as a continuum of specified behaviors from zero performance to

conspicuous excellence and place any given performance somewhere along that continuum.[*] For example, if ice skating was chosen as the clearly specified set of behaviors, then we could imagine a zero point as "Can't stand alone on ice." Conspicuous excellence at the other end of the continuum might be "Completes triple axel with perfect landing." A triple axel is a specific set of behaviors that judges can agree on with near perfect uniformity. In between zero and the triple axel are intermediate levels of accomplishment. The standards for these accomplishments (the criteria of CRT) can also be described and the performance of the skater evaluated in reference to them.

The world of education is somewhat vaguer and more complex, but the concept of CRTs generated a great deal of enthusiasm. The notion of CRTs, in the words of Cornell University psychometrician Jason Millman, "totally destroyed the monopoly of norm-referenced interpretations that was held in many quarters." In 1994, Millman reflected on how he and many others reacted to the concept of a CRT:

> Thirty years ago I was a young pup, full of ambition and optimism. I thought that if only educators could write good test specifications, explicitly stating what was and was not part of the content coverage, CRTs would be able to meet their promise. More than that, even, I believed CRTs could give quantitative interpretations such as: Billy can answer 65% of the questions contained in a given domain. But I was wrong.[10]

Millman's enthusiasm and subsequent disillusionment were common. What happened? Basically, the testers found that they couldn't specify educational outcomes with the clarity that they could specify the outcomes of ice skating. Ice skating is easy to observe, but what's in a kid's head is not. It is also difficult to infer from a test precisely what the student knows. More important, ice skating is a

---

[*] Glaser invented the term, but Edward L. Thorndike described almost precisely the same concept some 50 years earlier.

very limited range of behaviors. The goals of education are more general.

Although criterion-referenced tests became all the rage in the 1970s, they had a problem: they had no criteria. Or, more precisely, a "criterion" was imposed on the test through the act of setting a "cut score" for passing or failing. Thus the "criterion" for many minimum competency tests was a certain score, say 60, called the cut score. Above this you pass. Below this you fail. This is hardly the kind of criterion Glaser had in mind. It reduced criterion-referenced tests to nothing more than norm-referenced tests without the norm. The use of cut scores has itself been controversial and problematic, particularly in the use of "minimum competency" or other tests to determine grade promotion or eligibility for graduation.

Such tests were tests of "minimal" skills or "essential" skills and so gave the impression that all test-takers should attain perfect scores, otherwise they would fail in life. So what did it mean, then, to set a cut score at, say, 60% correct, a commonly used figure?

More troublesome was the mere notion of minimum competency. Should a student who scored 61% be permitted to graduate while a student who scored 59% was forced to repeat his entire senior year or receive something less than a diploma?

Such decisions are particularly troubling in view of the existence of something the test-makers call "measurement error." No test is perfectly accurate. If you gave a student a test, then somehow obliterated his memory of it and gave it to him again the next day, it is most unlikely that he would obtain precisely the same score. The measurement error of a test can be estimated statistically, and for a number of tests used for promotion/retention decisions or graduation eligibility, it is quite large. Good practice would require that this error at least be taken into account in setting a cut score. But real practice seldom emulates good practice, in part because these tests emerged largely from political concerns rather than educational concerns.

These kinds of issues concerning cut scores were never really resolved — they are, in fact, not resolvable by technical means although taking measurement error into account is technically useful. The issues were resolved in practice by setting the cut scores high enough to ensure that enough students initially failed to satisfy those who had called for the tests in the first place, but low enough that very few students would not pass by the time of their graduation. The students who still could not pass were further protected from humiliation by receiving a "certificate of completion" or something similar, in a fashion that the audience at the graduation ceremony would not know it was not a diploma.

In the years since the initial popularity of CRTs and minimum-competency testing programs, the sanctions for not passing the tests have stiffened. In Maryland, for instance, students who do not pass the state tests get nothing. Virginia is moving toward a similar program. In North Carolina, students in the class of 1998 who do not score above a certain level on that state's tests will be denied diplomas, and there is a move afoot to use the tests at lower grades for promotion and retention decisions.[*]

Before leaving this chapter, we should observe that the difference between an NRT and a CRT is one of usage and interpretation, not a necessary distinction. Seldom does one test serve both purposes well, but it would be possible to collect norms for a CRT, and it is possible, albeit very difficult, to give a criterion-referenced interpretation to NRTs.

---

[*] The concept of minimum competency itself stirred tremendous controversy within the testing community. Ultimately it was realized that such a concept could not be specified by technical, psychometric methodology. The answer to the question, "How much is enough?" is always arbitrary whether one is referring to a cut score on a minimum-competency test or to a college entrance test or to an examination for admission to medical practice. It must be kept in mind, though, that "arbitrary" has two meanings. Most commonly, it means "capricious." But it also refers to arbitration. In setting standards for any kind of test, it is important that arbitration be sufficient that there is some agreement and some reasonableness to the standards.

CHAPTER 4

Performance Tests

situations in which a student had to select one of the alternatives provided by the test-maker. These tests were a type of performance test, and performance test is probably a better generic term so we'll go with that.

Performance tests, for the most part, are not "standardized" in the ways that the tests we discussed in the preceding chapter are "standardized." When all students respond to the same writing "prompt" in a writing assessment, then some amount of standardization is involved, especially if they must all finish in a given amount of time and are given no opportunity later to edit and revise. But performance tests introduce a degree of idiosyncrasy into the assessment situation.[*]

Performance tests are one kind of criterion-referenced test that directly measures the performance the assessor is interested in. For example, music competitions, auditions, portfolios, athletic contests all directly measure the skills of interest.

Beginning in the late 1980s, some people in the assessment field did more than just express frustrations over the limits of multiple-choice tests. They began experimenting with tests that actually required students to perform. These tests became known popularly as "authentic tests" although some objected to this name because it implied that other forms of testing were "inauthentic" or phony. The term authentic was used because they required students to solve authentic problems from the real world, not

---

[*] As an aside, note that a number of people prefer to use the word "assessment" when referring to a performance test. The English word "assessment" comes from an old French word and is related to the modern French verb *s'assoir,* to sit oneself down. The idea is that, while a test might be done by "remote control," an assessment requires the assessor to sit down beside the student, much as a doctor might sit down next to a patient. It is only in this more intimate and intense context that the assessor can really assess the student's performance. In the following discussion, I use "test" and "assessment" interchangeably.

Why are performance tests so seldom seen in schools? There are several reasons. In all the examples of performance testing listed, only small numbers of people are involved at any one time. Performance tests take a lot of time and money to administer and score. If the goal of an assessment can be reached by using the much faster, much cheaper multiple-choice tests, then there is little reason to spend the extra time, effort, and money on performance assessments. And recall that, in the history of testing in this country, the emphasis has been on making discriminations among people, not on determining how well they actually perform. Paper-and-pencil tests can spread people out on bell curves much faster and cheaper than performance measures. Similarly, if the interest is in obtaining some idea of how well a school or, more likely, a school system, is functioning, the use of performance assessments would be horrendously expensive and time-consuming.

However, there are many aspects of education (and life) that do not lend themselves well to multiple-choice tests. The most obvious school-related area has already been mentioned, writing. One cannot measure writing skills by means of multiple-choice questions. More important, children cannot learn to write by practicing the editing skills that can be assessed through multiple-choice tests. Children must actually write to learn how to write. This statement seems so obvious that one wonders why it was ignored for so long.

Here is one reason why: Traditional testers would point out that writing assessments using actual writing and "writing" assessments using multiple-choice questions were highly correlated, so why bother with the more expensive, time-consuming writing? This is an adequate response *only* in situations where one wishes to make discriminations among students. Since that is what traditional testing has been all about, the response is not surprising. But the correlation between the two types of tests tells you only that those who score high on the multiple-choice test tend to score high on the writing test. "Scoring high," however, tells you nothing about the *quality* of the performance.

"Scoring high" tells you only about the performance of students in relation to each other — it's a normative statement. It could easily be that the writing of all students is awful but those who score higher than their peers on one form of the test score higher than their peers on the other form.

The statement "children must write to learn how to write" illustrates another aspect of good testing: good testing does not simply measure performance, it informs it. People can learn something from it. Not much can be learned from taking a multiple-choice test. Consider the following questions:

What is the volume of a cone that has a base area of 78 square centimeters and a height of 12 centimeters?

a. 30 cm^3 c. 936 cm^3
b. 312 cm^3 d. 2,808 cm^3

This is a fairly typical multiple-choice item borrowed from Grant Wiggins' *Assessing Student Performance* that might occur on a geometry test. Several of these questions would provide some idea of how well students know the formulas for calculating volumes of different shapes, although they would provide no information about why students had chosen the answers they picked. Moreover, each such question is a decontextualized question. That is, it has no real-life context, no way for the student to know why the formulas are important. In contrast, consider this performance task:

Background. Manufacturers naturally want to spend as little as possible not only on the product, but on packaging it and shipping it to stores. They want to *minimize* the cost of their packaging and they want to *maximize* the amount of what is packaged inside (to keep handling and postage costs down: the more individual packages you ship, the more it costs).

Setting: Imagine that your group of two or three people is one of many in the packaging department responsible for packing M & M candies for shipment. The manager of the shipping department has found that the cheapest material for shipping comes as a flat piece of rectangular paperboard (the piece of posterboard you will be given). She is asking each group in the packaging department to help solve this problem: *What completely closed container, built out of the given piece of posterboard, will hold the largest volume of M & M candies for safe shipping?*

1. Prove, in a convincing written report to company executives, that both the shape and the dimensions of your group's container maximize the volume. In making your case, supply all important data and formulas. Your group will also be asked to make a three-minute oral report at the next staff meeting. Both reports will be judged for accuracy, thoroughness, and persuasiveness.

2. Build a model (or multiple models) out of the posterboard of the proposed container shape and size that you think solves the problem. The models are not proof; they illustrate the claims that you offer in your report.

Here we have a real-life, challenging problem, also borrowed from Grant Wiggins' *Assessing Student Performance.* Students must be able to justify their answers. They must work with others. They actually have to structure part of the problem themselves. Knowing formulas is necessary, but not sufficient.

This problem meets the criteria of the "new basics" as described by economists Richard Murnane of Harvard and Frank Levy of MIT in their 1996 book, *Teaching the New Basics.* Murnane and Levy analyzed the requirements for jobs that would pay at least a middle-class wage. They settled on six skills, only two of which are actually new in terms of what people have proposed that schools should teach. One is "the ability to solve semi-structured problems where hypotheses must be formed and tested." The other is "the ability to work in groups with persons of various backgrounds." I would add to the list "the ability to communicate effectively, both orally and in writing."

These three skills look important beyond the narrow confines of the workplace. For instance, when you buy a car (or a house), you have to structure the problem in terms of how many passengers you need room for, how much money you can afford to spend, how much fun you want the car to be to drive, what kind of mileage you want to get from it, and a host of other factors. One of the biggest aids in solving any problem is to be able to accurately frame the problem.

Schooling should be, in part, about teaching people to think. The ability to critically evaluate information is crucial to functioning in a democratic society

Some have argued that multiple-choice tests can test higher-order thinking skills. It is certainly true that such tests *can* test higher-order thinking skills, but they rarely do. Usually multiple-choice tests that require thinking are found in a limited range of courses in graduate school. Indeed, most tests *punish* the thinking test-taker. Thinking takes time. And as a test-taker, the last thing you want while taking most tests is something that slows you down the way thinking does.

We can see the import of thinking and the difficulty of using multiple-choice tests by describing higher-order thinking. Lauren Resnick, a cognitive psychologist at the University of Pittsburgh has listed some of the qualities of higher-order thinking:

Higher-order thinking

1. is nonalgorithmic. That is, the path of action is not fully specified in advance [this is analogous to having to structure a problem].
2. tends to be complex. The total path is not "visible" (mentally speaking) for any single vantage point.
3. often yields multiple solutions, each with costs and benefits, rather than unique solutions.
4. involves nuanced judgment and interpretation.
5. involves the application of multiple criteria, which sometimes conflict with one another.
6. often involves uncertainty. Not everything that bears on the task at hand is known.

7. involves self-regulation of the thinking process. We do not recognize higher-order thinking in an individual when someone else "calls the plays" at every step.
8. involves imposing meaning, finding structure in apparent disorder.
9. is effortful. There is considerable mental work involved in the kinds of elaborations and judgments required.[11]

A student who deploys higher-order thinking of this kind while taking the SAT is in trouble. Time will expire before the test has been completed. The reader might want to match these qualities of higher-order thinking against the requirements of the M & Ms problem described earlier.

Students solving the M & Ms problem — taken from a real class in a real school — would also learn something in the process. The assessment would inform as well as measure.

In another publication, Lauren Resnick, along with her husband, historian Daniel Resnick, looked at what schools have required of children over the history of the nation.[12] They observe that only

recently have American schools been expected to impart this kind of higher-order thinking to *all* students.[*]

Performance tests are not without their problems, aside from their costs in time and money. For instance, while the outcomes of the M & Ms problem are fairly straightforward, there are ambiguities in the use of portfolios. Portfolios are used in a number of schools and districts as the major portion of writing assessment. Decisions have to be made as to what goes into a portfolio: the student's best work or the student's typical work? The teacher's selection of "best work" or the student's? How many writing types? Students with an aptitude for narration might want to concentrate on stories, ignoring essays, technical reports, and poetry. Who grades the portfolio? Different teachers judge the same work differently. While this last has been considered largely in terms of teacher unreliability, it probably also reflects genuine philosophical differences. One solution to this problem has been to train teachers to judge certain aspects of writing in similar ways. But does this cause them to overlook other meaningful qualities of the writing?

If the work is done in a group, but grades are to be assigned to individuals, the question arises as to whose work it is. Some parents object to group projects, alleging that a few kids end up doing all the work. Other parents accept the practice as good preparation for real life.

Multiple-choice tests will no doubt continue to flourish. For accountability and differentiation among students, it is hard to see how performance tests can replace them. Parents, though, it seems to me, should be concerned that performance tests become part of their children's educational experiences. An education geared only to the skills that are tested by commercial achievement tests, the SAT, and similar tests will be schooling aimed at the traditional goals of mass education.

---

[*] "Traditionally, an education developing these qualities of thinking was reserved for America's elite. 'Mass education,' from its inception, was designed to teach routine abilities: simple computation, reading predictable texts, and reciting religious or civic codes. It had nothing to with reading texts that needed to be interpreted; it had no notion that students themselves could create texts that others might need or want to read; it had no notion that students would need to solve semistructured problems, form hypotheses, or otherwise show creativity in developing original solutions."

Some recent research suggests that many Americans are still receiving a traditional mass education. An analysis of videotapes of mathematics instruction in Japan, Germany, and the United States found American teachers spending much more time teaching algorithms and procedures, while German and, especially, Japanese teachers tended to concentrate on conceptual understanding.

CHAPTER 5

Interpreting Test Scores

We have talked about test scores mostly in terms of percentile ranks, but ranks are not the only way of reporting test scores. Other ways include grade-equivalents, normal-curve equivalents, standard scores, and stanines. All of these scales are mathematically related to the normal curve shown in Figure 2. Let's take a brief look at each of these in turn.

Grade-Equivalents. Teachers and parents love grade-equivalents. They have such an intuitive appeal. If Suzy is in the third month of the third grade and gets a grade-equivalent of 3.3 on a test, the teacher can tell the parents that Suzy is "at grade level," and the parents can go home thinking that Suzy is where she should be for her age. But, like a national norm, 50% of all children are by definition below "grade level."

Test-makers define "grade level" as the score of the average student in a particular grade. A student in the third month of the third grade who obtains the "grade level" score gets a grade-equivalent of 3.3. Remember, by this definition, 50% of all

students, nationally, are below grade level. This kind of definition can lead to a lot of mischief if, as has happened, a newspaper reports that 30% of the members of a graduating class in a high school are not reading at grade level. People who are not aware of how test publishers define grade-equivalent will assume, quite naturally, that all of the graduating seniors should be reading at grade level. And if they aren't, what on earth is the high school doing giving them diplomas? But, to repeat, half of all students in the nation will be below grade level — by definition.

Further — and more common — mischief often occurs when a child in, say, the fourth grade, brings home a test report declaring that she has a grade-equivalent in reading of 7. Why, the parents are likely to wonder, is my child not in seventh grade, at least for her reading, since she is reading at seventh-grade level?

But she is *not* reading at seventh-grade level. The seventh-grade level for seventh-graders is the score that the average seventh-grader would score on seventh-grade reading material. When a fourth-grader gets a grade equivalent of 7 on a test, it represents what the average seventh-grader would score *on fourth-grade reading material.*[*]

Still more trouble arises when people average grade-equivalents. They look like they can be averaged. After all, they're numbers, aren't they? Grade-equivalents may look like any other numbers, but they are not. Scientists talk of scales as having different properties that determine what can be done with them mathematically. In ascending order of precision, these scales are nominal, ordinal, equal interval, and equal ratio. A scale must attain the status of "equal interval" before its numbers can be meaningfully averaged.

> But, to repeat, half of all students in the nation will be below grade level — by definition.

In an "equal interval" scale the distance between one number and the next is always the same. In such a scale numbers can be averaged. Temperature, whether in degrees Celsius or Fahrenheit, is such a scale. Each degree represents the same amount of heat. Taking one temperature reading of 60° and another of 40° and calculating an average of 50° is reasonable and gives a meaningful result. But averaging grade-equivalents is more like averaging house numbers (an ordinal scale). They are not part of an equal interval scale. You know that 608 S. Elm Street is farther south than 604 S. Elm, but 606 S. Elm (the average), might be quite close to 608 and quite far away from 604.

Percentiles. We have already discussed percentiles in passing, but we should mention here that they are not an equal interval scale, either. In terms of distance along the normal curve, a gain from the 50th

---

[*] Of course, this would be true only if any seventh-graders had ever taken the fourth-grade test. But they haven't. Test publishers cannot afford too much out-of-grade testing, such as giving the fourth-grade test to seventh-graders. Mostly, they give the fourth-grade test to some sample of third-graders and fifth-graders. The projection of how a typical seventh-grader would score is a statistical extrapolation based on the scores of third-, fourth-, and fifth-graders. We have no idea how valid it might be in reality.

percentile to 60th is much smaller than a gain from 80th to 90th. This is shown below in Figure 2.

Normal-Curve Equivalents. The normal-curve equivalent (NCE) was developed to try and remedy the problems discussed above concerning grade-equivalents and percentile ranks. The NCE was an attempt to create an equal interval scale for testing. Instead, it just created incomprehensibility. If your student scores at the 60th percentile, you know he did better than 60% of the kids in the population tested. If he gets an NCE of 60, you could learn, by looking at the normal curve below, that he scored better than 68% of the other students. For a percentile rank, you don't need to look at the normal curve. But an increase of your child's NCE from 60 to 70 doesn't mean that he scored better than 78% of the students. It means he scored better than 83% of the other kids — something you could learn only by looking at the normal curve again. Well, you could memorize all of these numbers, but no one bothers when percentile ranks give them to you automatically.

It would be something else if NCEs had what psychometricians call "construct validity." If, say, an increase from an NCE of 50 to 60 meant an increase in some defined psychological trait and if an increase from 60 to 70 meant the same amount of increase, then NCEs would take on new life and form a true equal interval scale. But they don't have any construct validity, because their origins

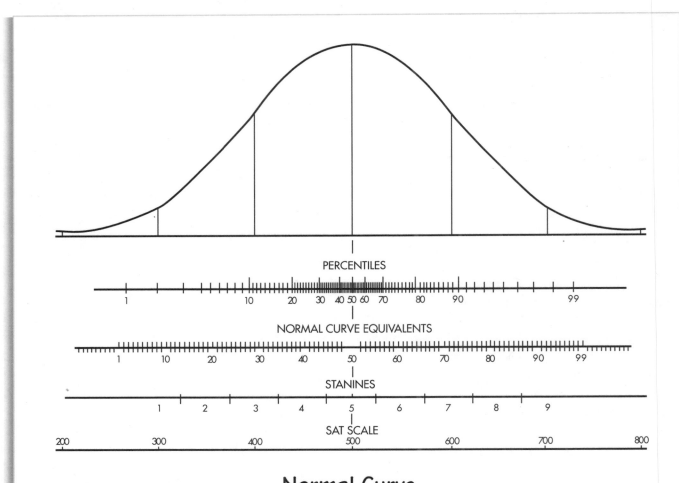

Normal Curve
FIGURE 2

were purely statistical. They were not developed in connection with any construct, such as intelligence, ability, achievement, or anything else. All you can know about NCEs is that bigger is better.

Standard Scores. In a way, standard scores are the most technical of the various types of scores, but they are also the most familiar. An IQ score is a standard score. So is the score on the SAT, ACT, NAEP, GRE, LSAT, GMAT, and so forth. Almost all commercial achievement tests come with some scale referred to as a "growth scale" or "developmental scale." These, too, are standard scores. Unlike percentile ranks which tell you only where your child stands in regard to other children, standard scores permit you to see how much progress your child has made between, say, third and fourth grades. School districts seldom make use of these kinds of standard scores.

All of the standard scores listed above begin life as a scale defined in terms of standard deviations and the normal curve. Suppose we have a bunch of test scores whose mean is 50 and whose standard deviation is 10. Then consider the selected set of scores: 20, 30, 40, 50, 60, 70, 80.

Suppose we take each of these scores, subtract the mean from it, and divide by the standard deviation. Here is what would happen to, say, a score of 80. If the mean is 50 and the standard deviation is 10, then a score of 80 is 30 points — three standard deviations — above the mean. And when we subtracted the mean and divided by the standard deviation, we got a new score in terms of standard deviation units: $(80-50)/10 = +3$. The whole set of sample scores would look like this:

- $(20-50)/10 = -3$
- $(30-50)/10 = -2$
- $(40-50)/10 = -1$
- $(50-50)/10 = 0$
- $(60-50)/10 = +1$
- $(70-50)/10 = +2$
- $(80-50)/10 = +3$

For all tests the standard scores, called z scores, will always range between -3 and +3. They are scores that measure a person's position on the normal curve.[*] And +3 means three standard deviations above the mean. Easy to remember. Much easier than juggling all those means and standard deviations for each test.

But, we just said that IQ scores and SAT scores are standard scores, and these scores don't look anything like IQ or SAT scores. True, but we can get from what we have to those scores easily. Let's take each z score, multiply by 15 and add 100. A z score of 0 — the mean — becomes 0 x 15 + 100 = 100. A z score of +3 becomes 3 x 15 + 100 = 145,

---

[*] You could know this position by keeping in mind the mean and standard deviation, but each new test would have a different mean and a different standard deviation, and the whole process of thinking about where a person is on the normal curve would be very cumbersome indeed.

And if you don't keep the standard deviation in mind for each test, the results can be misleading. Suppose Mary scored 70% correct on the first test of the year and 73% on the second. She did better on the second, right? Well, by one criterion, percent correct, yes. And if we are grading on an absolute scale, that's all we need. But if we're "grading on the curve" or simply want to know Mary's position relative to other students, we're in the dark.

We don't yet know the average scores so we can't tell if her score is better or worse than the average. Let's assume that the average was 60 on the first test and 65 on the second. Now it begins to look like, relatively speaking, she did better on the first test than on the second, scoring 10% correct above average on the first, but only 8% better on the second. But let us further suppose that the standard deviation was 5 on the first test and 10 on the second. That makes Mary +2 S.D. on the first test — (70-60)/5. Only 2% of the students will score higher (Mary scores better than the 50% below average, better than the 34% between the mean and +1 S.D., and better than the 14% between +1 S.D. and +2 S.D.; these add up to 98%). But her performance on the second test makes her only +.8 S.D. above the mean — (73-65)/10. She only scored better than 79% of the students on test 2.

and so forth. The distribution of scores now looks like this: 55, 70, 85, 100, 115, 130, 145.

Now these are beginning to look a lot more like IQ scores: they have a mean of 100 and a standard deviation of 15. They could have a mean of 50 and a standard deviation of 5 — the choice of scale is completely arbitrary.[*]

The conversion from raw scores to z scores does not change the relationship of the scores to one another in any way. If I know that a person got a z score of + 1, I know he did better than 84% of the rest of the test-takers. How do I know this? Well, 50% of the scores fall below the mean (assuming a normal distribution here so that the mean, median, and mode are all the same). And 34% of all scores will fall between the mean and + 1 standard deviation.

This is discussed in the technical section on the normal curve but is mostly something that needs to be memorized. Thirty-four percent of all scores will fall between the mean and +1 or -1 standard deviation. Another 14% will fall between +1 and +2 standard deviations and -1 and -2 standard deviation. So, in all normal curves, 96% of all scores will fall between -2 and +2 standard deviations. Check the normal curve graph on page 32 to see a visual representation of this.

This exposition on standard scores is presented not because they are magical or in any way mysterious.

---

[*]When you multiply by a constant or add a constant to a set of test scores, you are performing what statisticians call a "linear transformation" on the numbers, a transformation that does nothing to alter the relationship of the numbers (if you squared any of the numbers or took the square root of any or raised any to some higher power, you'd be making non-linear transformations and some relationships would change). When the College Board built the SAT it wanted a scale that could not be confused with any other set of scores. So the statisticians simply took their z scores, multiplied by 100 and added 500. A z score of 0 is the z score of the mean raw score. Then, 0 x 100 + 500 = 500, the average score on the SAT. *Voilà*, a scale with a mean of 500 and a standard deviation of 100.

Indeed, my purpose is just the opposite: to remove the mystery. Standard scores are used everywhere, so it is a good idea to have some notion of where they come from and how they can be interpreted.

Stanines. Stanine is short for "standard nine." Each stanine represents a certain percentage of the normal curve as follows:

Stanine

| 1 | 2 | 3 | 4 | 5 | 6 | 7 | 8 | 9 |

Percentage

| 4 | 7 | 12 | 17 | 20 | 17 | 12 | 7 | 4 |

Thus the bottom 4% of the scores are the first stanine; the top 4%, the ninth.

Stanines are seldom used anymore, and people might be hiding something if they use stanines. It is common practice to consider the fourth, fifth, and sixth stanines, the three stanines in the middle, as "average." If you add up these three stanines, you get 54% of the scores. These can be reported as average. The seventh, eighth, and ninth stanines contain another 23% of the scores. So if you are an enterprising school public relations official, you can tell the media that 77% (54% + 23%) of your students are average or above average! Only the bottom 23% of the scores — those in the first, second, and third stanines — need be reported as "below average."

Let's assume your school district is perfectly "normal" and that its average score is the same as the national norm — the 50th percentile. If your district reported its test scores in percentile ranks, 50% of the students would be below average. But if the percentile ranks are collapsed into stanines, only those with a percentile rank of 23 or below would be reported as below average.

What follows are actual test scores for several students. Examine them carefully. How do you react to them? How do you interpret them? My comments on these numbers follow the student scores.

CTBS/4 Comprehensive Tests of Basic Skills, Fourth Edition

Comprehensive Tests of Basic Skills

STUDENTS	SCORES	READING Vocab	READING Compr	READING Total	LANGUAGE Mech	LANGUAGE Expr	LANGUAGE Total	MATHEMATICS Compu	MATHEMATICS C & A	MATHEMATICS Total	Total Battery +	WORD ANLYS
Student #1	NP	65	45	54	71	59	63	43	55	50	55	14
DOB: 6/24/88 Age: 8-10	NS	6	5	5	6	5	6	5	5	5	5	3
	GE	3.3	2.7	2.9	3.4	3.2	3.3	2.7	2.9	2.8	2.9	X
Form: A Level: 12	NCE	58	47	52	62	55	57	47	53	50	53	27
	AANCE	39	38	38	38	39	38	43	47	45	40	42
Student #2	NP	*99	99	99	75	92	85	*99	99	99	99	90
DOB: 5/4/89 Age: 7-11	NS	9	9	9	6	8	7	9	9	9	9	8
	GE	9.1	12.+	11.3	3.5	6.6	4.9	4.7	10.7	6.4	7.1	X
Fomr: A Level: 12	NCE	99	99	99	64	79	72	99	99	99	99	77
	AANCE	81	85	84	75	84	79	70	77	75	83	75
Student #3	NP	55	75	65	4	63	27	54	43	49	46	76
DOB: 4/18/89 Age: 8-0	NS	5	6	6	1	6	4	5	5	5	5	6
	GE	3.0	4.0	3.4	1.0	3.4	2.3	2.8	2.6	2.8	2.7	X
Form: A Level: 12	NCE	53	64	58	14	57	37	52	47	49	48	65
	AANCE	57	55	56	53	56	55	52	56	54	55	56

TEST OF COGNITIVE SKILLS SECOND EDITION

	Scores	NON VRB	VRB	TOT
NPA	47	59	17	36
NPA	93	87	98	98
NPA	77	78	73	80

NORMS FROM: 1988
TEST DATE: 4/7/97
SCORING: PATTERN (IRT)
QUARTER MONTH: 31
CITY: SCHOOL:
STATE: DISTRICT:

+ Total Battery includes Total Reading, Total Language, and Total Mathematics.
NP: NATIONAL PERCENTILE
NS: NATIONAL STANINE
GE: GRADE EQUIVALENT
NCE: NORMAL CURVE EQUIVALENT
AANCE: ANTICIP. NORM. CURVE EQUIV.

*:   MAXIMUM OR MINIMUM SCORE
X: NO SCORE AVAILABLE
NPA: NATL PERCENTILE BY AGE
CSI: COGNITIVE SKILLS INDEX

Adapted version of Class Record Sheet reproduced with written permission of the McGraw-Hill Companies, Inc.

My Comments:

The first thing I would want to know is how the CTBS tests the various components. There are different kinds of skills that can be called "language mechanics" or "language expression." And there are different possible formats for the items. I'd want to see precisely what this test is testing.

The results give a full array of test scores and ranks, and the page defines what each of the scores' abbreviations means. The "national percentile" means that these children's scores are being compared to a national sample, not to the norms for urban students or suburban, etc. This might or might not be the most revealing. If the school is located in a quite wealthy suburb, we

would expect high scores relative to the nation as a whole, and it might be more appropriate to see how this wealthy school stacks up against other wealthy schools. The sheet also provides stanines, grade-equivalents, normal curve equivalents, and something called "anticipated normal curve equivalents." I will come back to this last measure in a moment.

The variety of scores allows you to choose whichever metric you feel most comfortable with — none of these scores is going to contradict another in terms of what it shows about the child. If the student is above average on one of them, she'll be above average on all. If this were not true, the scores wouldn't really make any sense.

Student 1 has a range of percentile ranks from 43 to 71 (on the individual tests). Is this "normal"? Probably and especially for younger children. Learning is not linear and young children are not nearly as "standardized" as older ones. Many school systems don't begin testing children until the third grade so we likely don't know what this child's scores looked like in previous years. As noted in the text, though, bouncing around some 25 percentile ranks over a four-year period is not that uncommon.

Student 2 shows an almost unbroken string of "99's" in the percentile rank row. He's a little weaker in the language area. I wouldn't be alarmed at this, but would note it for future observation. It's a little unusual to see the student in the 99th percentile when one test, language, is at the 85th, but this indicates that other students had similar patterns, obtaining a less than 99 on some individual test. This child's total score would be boosted by the fact that he has an extremely high 99 in reading comprehension. Not all 99th percentiles are alike. An 800 is a perfect score on the SAT and, of course, it places you at the 99th percentile. But so few people get an 800 that the among the top 1% of the scorers (those who make up the 99th percentile), are some students with scores of 750, 760, 770, 780, and 790 (on the old scale).

The grade-equivalent is one of those ridiculous extrapolations that can be misleadingly interpreted as indicating that this child is reading better than a high school senior. It is also curious that the 99th percentile for vocabulary has an asterisk next to it indicating a maximum possible score while comprehension has no such asterisk. Yet, the results on the grade-equivalent scale are much higher for comprehension (12. +) than for vocabulary (9.1). I'd want some explanation for this, but if the school system is not large enough to have a psychometrician in the central office, an explanation might be hard to find.

Student 3 presents a challenge. We see a mostly consistent pattern of percentile ranks, but a 4th percentile on language mechanics. Coupled with a 63 on language expression, this is surprising. The first thing I would want to do with these results is check the child's answer sheet. Young children sometimes answer two questions on one row of bubbles or skip a question, either of which throws their entire pattern of answers off. This could easily be the cause of the low score.

After that, I'd want to know if the child spoke English as his native language. It is not likely that a native language other than English would yield a 4 in mechanics and a 63 in expression, but it is possible.

After checking these possibilities, I'd want to look around for other evidence that the child has some kind of impairment when dealing with language. We don't see any on this page and might want to speak with the parents.

On the right of the page are results for the "Test of Cognitive Skills," which is the "ability" test that partners with the CTBS. I'm not sure what the "verbal" section of this test actually tests, but it shows no language deficiency.

The Cognitive Skills Index, by the way, is some calculation which combines all three subtests. I imagine that it is very much like an IQ scale with a mean of 100 and a standard deviation of 15, and I would predict it to correlate very highly with an actual IQ test from the Stanford Binet or other similar test.

About that "anticipated normal curve equivalent." From the scores over on the right hand side of the page, the cognitive skills scores, a formula is used to predict how well the child will do on each of the achievement tests. We could just as easily use the achievement test scores to predict the "ability" test scores. This is the kind of prediction that leads to the unfortunate labeling of some children as over- or underachievers.

The prediction here is made for NCE's, but it could just as well have been made for any of the other scores except stanines, which are too crude a scale.

CHAPTER 6

Specific Tests

So far, we have talked about tests in general. It is worthwhile, though, to discuss a few specific tests that are highly visible and very influential either on life decisions or education policy matters. We will describe the Iowa Tests of Basic Skills, a commercial norm-referenced achievement test, but this description will suffice to describe achievement tests in general. Most of what is said about the ITBS can be applied to the other widely used achievement tests: the Comprehensive Tests of Basic Skills, the Stanford Achievement Tests, the Metropolitan Achievement Tests, and the California Achievement Tests.

We will also consider the Scholastic Assessment Test (known from 1926 to 1996 as the Scholastic Aptitude Test), the SAT. This is probably the best-known and most widely publicized test of recent years. Its less widely known college admissions cousin, the ACT, shares many of its features. The tests of the National Assessment of Educational Progress (NAEP) were largely invisible for many years but have recently come to strongly affect education policy throughout the nation. NAEP will be described in this chapter as will the multitude of IQ tests that play a significant role in the lives of individuals and debates about the nature of IQ that have reverberated in educational circles for almost a century.

THE IOWA TESTS OF BASIC SKILLS

The Iowa Tests of Basic Skills (ITBS) are available for testing children in kindergarten through grade 8. There are two additional sets of "Iowas" as they are often called, available for use in high school: the Tests of Achievement and Proficiency and the

Iowa Tests of Educational Development. The latter is a more difficult test with long reading passages, multi-step math problems, and simulated science experiments.

The basic core of the ITBS tests are the vocabulary, reading, language, and mathematics sections. Vocabulary items provide a boldface word in the context of a phrase and ask the child to select the word that is most like the boldface word. Reading passages include exposition, narrative, and poetry and, according to "A Message to Parents," "Some questions emphasize the understanding of stated information, but most questions require students to make inferences or draw generalizations."

The language section of the test is divided into four sections: spelling, capitalization, punctuation, and usage. In each, items present four lines of text, and the child's task is to pick which line contains an error. The fourth line is always *no mistakes* for use with items that contain no errors.

Mathematics is subdivided into math concepts and estimation, problem solving and data interpretation, and computation.[*] These divisions reflect the impact of both the National Council of Teachers of Mathematics Standards and the marketplace. The NCTM standards emphasize reasoning and problem solving and data interpretation.

In addition to this core battery, there are science and social studies subtests and sources of information, which is further divided into maps and diagrams. In some tests, the science and social studies sections contain a great deal of information that the questions ask about. This is a tradeoff. By putting the needed information in the material before the questions are asked, students without specific knowledge are not penalized, but the "science" test becomes something more of a "science reading" test.

The ITBS social studies test asks for specific information, such as "Which of these inventions made it practical to construct tall office buildings?" The options are the elevator, the automobile, glass window, and air conditioning. In science a question

might ask, "Which of these is a body part that helps the animal to catch its food?" The choices are a frog's sticky tongue, a monkey's long tail, a turtle's hard shell, a lion's thick mane. When the items do provide material, the answer cannot be obtained simply by reading the question:

> Andy poured 75 mL of water into a measuring cup. When he added a stone to the cup, the water level rose to 125 mL. What can be concluded from this information?
>
> A. The water weighs 200 mL. B. The stone takes up more space than the water does. C. The stone weighs more than the water. D. The stone has the same volume as 50 mL of water.

The idea behind the question, I imagine, is to test either the student's knowledge that a stone displaces a volume of water equal to its own volume or to test the student's ability to reason it out. However, this is a question that a student could get right without knowing about volume or without reasoning it through. If the student knows what mL

---

[*]At one time, the ITBS contained no computation test. The ITBS program developers at the University of Iowa felt that computation was the test most affected by the sequence of skills learned and the most subject to influence from speeded drills. They considered computation something best left to local discretion. However, the tests that test-makers make, get "adopted" (same wags say because they have no real home) by states, through a process of competitive bidding. The states specify what they want in a test, and the test publishers submit a bid trying to convince the state that their test best delivers what the state wants at the lowest price.

In 1976 the states of Texas and California, and several large cities, informed the ITBS developers that if their tests did not contain a computation test, they could not submit bids for those states' and cities' testing programs. California and Texas combined constitute a huge market. These two states have enough people in them to virtually control what test-makers put into their tests and so the Iowas added a computation test. In the 1980s the use and scoring of the computation test was made optional to users.

stands for, alternatives A and C are eliminated because they deal with weight and weight is not mentioned in the question's stem (the name for the part of the question that presents the information and question). If the student realizes that the level rose 50 mL (from 75 to 125 mL) and realizes that the water took up 75 mL, he can eliminate option B. He thus arrives at the right answer by elimination, never thinking about how a stone displaces water in terms of its own volume.

Alternatively, the student might simply reason that since the stem has numbers, the answer has to be in numbers. Two of the alternatives have numbers. One of these refers to weight, which is not mentioned in the stem. Therefore, the answer must be the other alternative. By this logic, the student gets the right answer with absolutely no thinking about volume.

The maps and diagrams section shows maps, flow charts, calendars, etc., and asks questions about their content, such as "Mary has to go to the doctor on May 4. What day of the week is that?" The sources of information section shows tables of contents in various guises.

THE SAT (Scholastic Assessment Test, née, Scholastic Aptitude Test) AND THE ACT

Where admission tests are concerned, this is widely perceived as the big one.

> The SAT is a series of tests that predict your ability to perform in the college environment by measuring the degree to which you possess knowledge that nobody in a million years would actually need.[13]

Few tests have attained the notoriety that the SAT has. It has been the subject of at least three highly critical books: *The Reign of ETS: The Corporation That Makes Up Minds,* by Allan Nairn and Ralph Nader; *None of the Above,* by David Owen; and *The Case Against the SAT,* by James Crouse and Dale Trusheim. Owen's book is by far the most accessible to the lay reader. Nairn and Nader rely

on some peculiar statistics, and Crouse and Trusheim's analysis, aside from the opening and closing chapters, is straightforward, but highly technical.

The often vilified SAT began life quietly enough. On November 17, 1900, administrators from a group of colleges and universities in the Northeast gathered at Columbia University in New York to deal with the problem of high school curricula. Students were arriving at these institutions of higher education with befuddling high school transcripts. The transcripts often indicated that the students had taken similar courses of study in high school when, in fact, the "same" courses reflected markedly different content. The colleges decided that they could bring some uniformity to the high school curriculum by giving tests in various subject areas. The content of the tests would tell high school teachers what the colleges valued.

We should note that the high school graduation rate in 1900 was about 10% and only a small percentage of those graduates went on to college. The colleges, nevertheless, had no qualms about dictating what the high school curriculum ought to look like.

Historically, fears that the colleges would reject students who had taken a non-traditional course of study have impeded innovation and reform in high schools. For example, in 1932 the Progressive Education Association (PEA) met and "in the course of the two-day discussion many proposals for the improvement of the work of our secondary schools were made and generally approved. But almost every suggestion was met with the question, 'Yes, that should be done in our high schools, but it can't be done without risking students' chances of being admitted to college'."[14]

The PEA's way around this barrier was to establish 30 what we might today call "break-the-mold" schools and to get colleges to waive their usual admissions requirements for eight years. The result

> The SAT "should be regarded merely as a supplementary record." Would that people had kept those words in mind over the years!

was known as "The Eight-Year Study" and the graduates of the 30 schools performed better academically than traditional students and were much more involved in the social and political life of the colleges. It is interesting to speculate on what impact the Eight-Year Study might have had had World War II not occurred at its end in 1940.

The colleges formed the College Entrance Examination Board to develop, administer, and, initially, score the tests. Although the phrase "measurement-driven instruction" did not become popular until the 1980s, the College Board (as it is usually referred to) was pushing it almost a century earlier. Having read reports of education reform commissions from later years, I conclude that the College Board did not accomplish its goal of rendering the high school curriculum coherent.

The scoring service was soon dropped when colleges complained about the imposition of having an outside authority determine their standards ("How dare they" was pretty much the reaction). The College Board's examinations were initially essay tests. The first tests were given in English, French, German, Latin, Greek, history, mathematics, and physics, and in the first year 973 students sat for these exams. In the second year, Spanish, botany, geography, and drawing were added, and the number of students rose to 1,362 (in 1997, it was 1,127, 021). Impressed with the

developments in testing during World War I, the College Board decided to develop a more general test that might predict who would succeed in college. In 1926 the Scholastic Aptitude Test (SAT) was born. Its developers were quite modest about what it could do. The SAT's principal architect, Carl Campbell Brigham, had this to say about it:

> The present state of all efforts of men to measure or in any way estimate the worth of other men, or to evaluate the results of their nurture, or to reckon their potential possibilities does not warrant any certainty of prediction.... This additional test now made available through the instrumentality of the College Entrance Examination Board may help to resolve a few perplexing problems, but it should be regarded merely as a supplementary record. To place too great emphasis on test scores is as dangerous as the failure to properly evaluate any score or rank in conjunction with other measures and estimates which it supplements.[15]

The SAT "should be regarded merely as a supplementary record." Would that people had kept those words in mind over the years! Actually, for many years the SAT was mostly a supplementary record. It was only after a long period of steady declines in SAT national averages that people began to look at the SAT in different ways.[*]

---

[*] There is no meaningful SAT "national average" although the College Board provides one each August. The percentage of seniors taking the SAT varies from 4% in Utah to 16% in Idaho to 49% in Washington to 60% in Indiana to 82% in Connecticut. It is not clear what all of these different percentages mean when averaged. Moreover, over the years the proportion of seniors taking the test has changed. Twenty years ago, about 30% of seniors took the SAT; currently 41% take it. The effect of differences in participation rates is discussed on page 46.

From the start, the SAT was divided into two sections, verbal and quantitative. The verbal section consisted of sentence completions, antonyms, analogies, and reading comprehension questions. The mathematics section consisted mostly of arithmetic, algebra, and geometry questions. A few questions on the mathematics section were designated as "other" types and included problems in inequalities, logic, intuitive topology, unusual symbols, operations, and definitions. The questions included both essay and multiple-choice items.

The onset of World War II interfered with the administration of the essay portion of the test in 1941, and from that time on the SAT was entirely multiple-choice, consisting of 85 items in the verbal section, 60 in the quantitative. Also in 1941 a new scale was adopted with the average score scaled to 500 (a standard score, discussed on pages 33-34), and the standard deviation — the measure of the variability of scores around the average — was set at 100. All subsequent administrations of the SAT were statistically equated to the 1941 administration in terms of difficulty, until 1996, when a "recentered" scale was adopted for reasons to be discussed momentarily.

It is important to know something about the students who set the original standards on the SAT, standards that were constant until 1996. They were 10,654 students from the Northeast. Ninety-eight percent of them were white, 60% were male, and fully 41% had attended private, college-prep high schools. They were, by any measure, an elite group. It was to the average score of this elite group that the scaled score of 500 was applied. In 1997, the SAT test-takers consisted of 1,127,021 students, 41% of the nation's entire senior class. They were 30% minority, 54% female, 83% public school attendees, and 26% from families with incomes of $30,000 or less. The pool of SAT test-takers has been truly democratized, but every one of these demographic changes is associated with lower test scores. It would have been astonishing — and very suspicious — if the average SAT scores had *not* declined. More about

this later. The score of 500, given to the average score of the 1941 elite, might have been representative of the average student wishing to attend college in 1941, but by 1996 it no longer was.

By 1950, the SAT verbal score had declined to 476, and it remained very stable around 475 until it began its notorious 20-year descent in 1963. No one speaks of this early decline, probably because no one can explain it. There were no large changes in curriculum between 1941 and 1950.[*] Very few television screens glowed in the nation's living rooms. And in those homes with televisions, 1950 marked the year before the beginning of a new situation comedy, "Ozzie and Harriet." These 1950s were the "togetherness" years of the Eisenhower Administration, and few people were worried about the decline of the family. Only jazz musicians and a few other marginalized groups were regularly using illegal drugs. Thus three powerful factors invoked to explain later declines — drugs, TV, and family decline — are not available as explanations for the first SAT score decline.

My guess is that it had something to do with the G.I. Bill, which permitted people to attend college who could not otherwise have afforded to do so. But we will never know for certain. In those days the College Board did not collect the kind of data it now gathers with the "Self-Descriptive Questionnaire" that now accompanies the SAT.

In any case, both the verbal and quantitative scores began to decline in 1963, a decline that lasted almost 20 years. In 1977 the College Board put together a panel to study the falling scores. The panel, headed by Willard Wirtz, former U.S. Secretary of Labor, and Harold Howe II, former U.S. Commissioner of Education, concluded that most of the decline from 1963 to 1970 was the result of changes in who was taking the test: more women, more minorities, more lower-income

---

[*] However, a large change was proposed in 1945 with the notion of a "life adjustment curriculum," but this curriculum was intended for the non-college bound.

students, and more students with low high school grade point averages. But, the panel claimed, those changes had stabilized by 1970, and other reasons needed to be found to explain the rest of the decline. (It's worth noting that some of the panel's staff disagreed that the demographics were stable in this second half of the decline.)

And did the panel ever find those reasons! One background paper for the panel simply listed the hypotheses that had been brought forward to explain the drop, all 76 of them. This works out to roughly one hypothesis for each point of decline. And the paper missed one of my favorites: that the decline occurred because of radioactive fallout from the nuclear testing program of the 1940s and 1950s.

Changes in curriculum, in teachers, in students, in the family, in religion, in civil rights, in values, in national priorities, in the economy, in technology, and in the population itself were all presented as candidates for causing the fall in SAT scores. The panel elected to go with some large societal disturbances in what it referred to as "a decade of distraction." Whether or not the demographics of test-takers were stable in the 1970s, the 1980s and 1990s brought large changes. Increasing numbers of Asian, Hispanic, and low-income students began to huddle in angst to bubble in answer sheets on Saturday mornings. When I conducted an analysis that took these changes in population into account, I determined that the verbal test had fallen only 22 points since 1951, while the quantitative, now usually referred to as the math section, had actually risen 5 points.[16]

Even without taking demographics into account, the mathematics section never showed a large decline. It fell into the 470s. Given the number of questions on the math section, this means that the average student in, say, 1983, when the decline ended, was getting about four fewer of the 60 items correct than in 1941. The fall in the SAT verbal from 1963 to 1983 represented about seven items.

We should note that, even if one accepts the decline without taking into account any demographic changes, the evidence indicates that the test score decline affected *only* the college-going population. All during the period when the SAT scores were falling, scores on the PSAT (Preliminary SAT) were stable. The PSAT is a short version of the SAT that is usually taken by high school sophomores. Periodically, a national norming study is conducted on a representative sample of all students who take the PSAT, and these national norming studies from 1964 to 1983 show no indication of change. In a national norming study, recall that students are selected so as to be representative of the whole nation. The SAT is taken only by those aspiring to attend certain colleges, and there is some indication that, as more and more students acquired such aspirations, the college-bound curriculum in high school was somewhat watered down.

Another decline in SAT scores has also been used by conservative school critics to claim that public education is in crisis. This is the decline in high-scorers. Not only did the average SAT score fall, the proportion of students scoring above 650 on the SAT verbal also fell. The proportion of those scoring above 650 on the SAT verbal declined from about 7% in the standard-setting group to just over 3% in the mid-1970s and has remained constant since then. Some of this decline, no doubt, occurred because a larger and larger proportion of the senior class has been taking the SAT. If one assumes that those scoring very high were always among those who were headed for college, then the increasing number of test-takers would be mostly made up of less able students, and those who score high would constitute a smaller proportion of this larger pool.

However, the absolute numbers of high scorers also fell. For instance, in 1966 and 1975, very similar numbers of students took the SAT. In 1966, 33,200 scored above 700 on the SAT verbal, but in 1975, only 15,900 had such scores. By 1995, the last year in which the old scale was used, the number was down to 12,800, but about 35% fewer students took the SAT in 1995 than in 1975. If the 1975 and 1995 groups had had the same number of test-takers, the 1995 group would have had 17,000 students scoring above 700, a slight increase over 1975, but still less than 1966.

Notice that all of the discussion of the decline of high scorers has been limited to the verbal section of the SAT. That is because the proportion of students scoring high on the quantitative section never declined much and, since 1981, has rebounded to become a record large group. In 1981, some 7% of the students were above 650, about the same as in the standard-setting group. By 1995, though, the proportion had grown to over 12% (an increase of about 75%). This is something that the school critics never mention.

Or, if they do, they claim that this growth is largely due to high-scoring Asian and Asian American students. It is not clear what point they are trying to make, but in any case they are wrong. It is true that Asian students score much higher on the quantitative section of the SAT than any other ethnic group, averaging 538 in 1995, the last year of the old scale. By comparison, whites, the next highest-scoring group, averaged 498 in that year. However, Asians constitute too small a proportion of the test population to account for much of the growth. As I noted above, between 1981 and 1995, the proportion of students scoring above 650 on the quantitative section of the SAT grew by about 75%. If the "Asian kids" hypothesis is true and if Asian students are removed from test-taking group, that 75% increase should disappear or at least become a lot smaller. However, with Asians held out of the sample, the proportion of high scorers still grows by 57%, so a lot more black, white, Hispanic, and Native American kids are scoring high in math, too.[*]

Does the SAT work? Well, before we can answer that question, we have to know exactly what it is supposed to do. The SAT is supposed to predict

success in the freshman year of college. Does it? Yes, but not as well as the College Board and the Educational Testing Service (ETS), which constructs, administers, and scores the SAT for the College Board, would have you believe. In one study, the SAT successfully predicted freshman grade-point averages no better than the scores from achievement tests. The Crouse and Trusheim book mentioned earlier also showed that the SAT improves the prediction made from high school grades and rank in class by only a tiny amount. It is, as its developer Brigham said in 1926, a mere supplement.

Is the SAT biased? There have been claims that the SAT is biased against both women and minorities.

---

[*] Such growth makes sense when one looks at the statistics for course-taking in mathematics and science: many more students in recent years have taken three and four years of these subjects than they did 15 years ago. I have been referring to the "old scale" and to the "recentering" that took place in 1996. You may be wondering what this is all about. Over the years since 1941, demographic changes meant that 500 no longer represented the score of the average college applicant. The 1941 standard-setters, who averaged 500, might have been an elite, but they were pretty well representative of who was seeking a college education in those days.

By 1996, though, 62% of all high school graduates were enrolled in some form of higher education in the following fall. The College Board decided to "recenter" the SAT scale, something that the publishers of achievement tests do every time they renorm a test. The College Board wanted 500 to once again represent the performance of the average test-taker. Using the 1941 scale, students receiving a score of 475 would naturally think that they were below average. And they were — but only in comparison to the 1941 elite who set the original standard. The recentering generated a storm of protest from conservative school critics. Chester E. Finn, Jr., a former Assistant Secretary of Education, called it the "biggest dose of educational Prozac" ever administered. Others claimed that the College Board was trying to hide low achievement. I think the critics were off target. If you want the average score of the SAT to reflect the score of the average student taking the test, the recentering makes sense.

The notion of bias against ethnic groups or lower socioeconomic status students arose over vocabulary words like "regatta." A regatta is more likely to be a part of the culture of affluent people, and knowing what the word means is more likely to reflect the cultural milieu than aptitude for college. There are statistical procedures for determining bias, and in recent years the claims of ethnic bias have died down.

Not so the claims of gender bias. No one really knows why women score lower on the SAT than men, even on the verbal section, but they do. The difference on the verbal score is tiny, four or five points each year on the SAT's 600-point scale. The math difference is much larger, 35 to 40 points depending on the year.

The difference also shows up on the PSAT and has an important practical outcome: the PSAT is the sole instrument used to qualify students for National Merit Scholarships. Each year about two-thirds of these scholarships go to males. This would be of no import if the higher SAT scores of males were followed by higher grade-point averages in college, but they aren't. One large study found a difference of 45 points between males and females on the SAT math section, but mostly small differences in college freshman math grades in favor of females, no matter whether the freshman math course was remedial, standard college, advanced algebra, or calculus. The National Merit Scholarship people have been singularly unresponsive to pleas to change the award process. They have refused to consider changes even though it has been pointed out that once we get to the semi-finalist level of selecting students, we are dealing with achievement levels so high that the prizes could be given *at random* and the quality of the students getting the awards would not decline.

Given the perceived importance of the SAT in college admissions, the question arises as to whether the SAT can be coached. Certainly two large corporations, Kaplan Educational Centers and The Princeton Review claim that it can be.

Unfortunately but understandably, these two firms have not substantiated their claims with the kinds of evidence that researchers will accept, nor have they been willing to permit researchers to conduct the kinds of experimental studies that would resolve the issue one way or another.

I discuss later (p. 52) that psychometricians sometimes act more like members of a religious order than like scientists. When I worked at ETS in the 1960s, it was revealed wisdom that the SAT was impervious to coaching. When a researcher showed that coaching was indeed feasible, ETS fired him.

Whether or not the SAT is coachable depends in part on how one defines "coaching." Most short-term instruction over a period of a week or so probably has little impact other than to revive dormant skills (e.g., a number of SAT math problems look impossible until one remembers how to factor equations, and they then become quite simple). The Princeton Review claims that its methods work by teaching students the "games" that ETS plays in item construction. I imagine this helps a little. The Kaplan Educational Centers rely more on prolonged contact with the SAT and SAT-like material. A question that is hard to answer is, When does prolonged contact cease to be coaching and become instruction?

Some item types would appear to be more coachable than others. Learning words and their antonyms, for instance, probably has little impact because of the small probability of encountering any specific word. On the other hand, practice in analogies might lead to the development of a more general skill. It would certainly teach a few "games." Most people approach analogies by seeking to solve them in terms of meaning, but for some analogy problems, meaning is irrelevant. For instance, pool: sleep as ?: peels. The alternatives might be loop, pool, sloop, spool. "Peels" is "sleep" in reverse, so the answer would be loop, "pool" reversed.

Something that is little noted is that the SAT has very little predictive validity beyond the first year of college. And for most colleges, the high school record remains a better predictor of college success than the SAT. Moreover, when combined with other parts of the high school record, the SAT adds very little to the ability of the colleges to predict who will succeed at their institutions.

As a "mere supplementary record," the SAT is mere indeed. At a few highly selective colleges, where most of the applicants have very high grades, the SAT does allow the schools to make finer discriminations — not all students with straight A's in high school will get the same SAT scores.

The value of the SAT has also been called into question by findings at schools that have made SAT scores optional for admission purposes. These schools do require SAT scores *after* admission for research, guidance, and placement purposes. Thus all students at these schools have SAT scores, but some didn't use them as part of their admissions application and others did.

Students who submit their SATs as part of their admissions package have total scores about 150 points higher than those who don't submit them. But — and it's a big but — their college grade-point averages don't differ from the non-submitters, and those who do not submit SATs don't leave school for academic reasons at any higher rate than those who sent their SATs to the dean of admissions. The nonsubmitters have turned out to be a more diverse group of applicants in terms of geographic area, ethnicity, and intended major (fine and performing arts majors are not typically great test-takers). Moreover, the faculties at the universities that have abandoned the SAT have pronounced themselves better satisfied with the more diverse student bodies that have resulted. (Think about it: a college full of high-scorers on the SAT would be a pretty awful environment; even colleges like Stanford and Harvard have a number of students with total scores of under 900.)

In sum, the SAT tells colleges precious little that they don't already know from other parts of a student's high school record. The College Board

and ETS have for many years promulgated the myth that the SAT can serve as a "common yard-stick" for all students. After all, it is a standardized test, and everyone takes it under the same circum-stances, while high school grades from the Bronx High School of Science and from South Succotash High might not reflect the same level of attain-ment. Yet it is also true that, despite this lack of comparability, the high school records of students from all over the country predict college success better than the SAT.

The myth of the "common yardstick" is also silly on its face. The test might be standardized, but the kids who take it definitely are not. Suppose we have one applicant at a college who comes from a wealthy, college-educated family, attends an elite college-prep high school, and scores 600 on the SAT verbal. Suppose we have another student who lives in an inner city with poor parents who never completed high school, attends the neighborhood public school, lacks a quiet place to study, works to help the family make ends meet, and scores 600 on the SAT verbal. Are these two students the same? Of course not. And college admissions officers know it. They will recruit the inner-city student like crazy and give the college-prep kid a ho-hum response (unless the parents are either wealthy or alumni or, preferably, both).

The "common yardstick" fantasy also serves to perpetuate another myth: that all applicants to a college are in competition with all other applicants. This has never been so. Colleges admit by cate-gories: the brains, the all-American kids, the special talents (athletes, artists, actors, musicians, etc.), the social conscience admits (perhaps an endangered species as more state laws take effect forbidding colleges to take ethnicity into account), the legacies (offspring of alumni), and the paying guests (those who don't need scholarship help).

Finally, in regard to the SAT, its state level results have been used to "prove" that money doesn't matter. Former Secretary of Education William Bennett put out a "report card" on American education and made such a claim. *Washington Post* pundit and fellow conservative, George Will, pounced on the study with a column titled, "Meaningless Money Factor." Will pointed out that the top five states, Iowa, North Dakota, South Dakota, Utah, and Minnesota were all low spenders. New Jersey, on the other hand, spent more money per kid per year than any other state and still only finished 39th in the great SAT race. What neither Will nor Bennett bothered to point out was that in the high-scoring states, few students take the SAT: they are all states that principally use the ACT. The percentages of students taking the SAT for the five states were 5, 6, 5, 4, and 10, respectively. The kids in Iowa who take the SAT are kids who want to leave Iowa and attend Harvard, Stanford, or some other highly selective school that requires the SAT. In New Jersey, on the other hand, fully 76% of the senior class bubbled in answer sheets for the College Board. It doesn't take an SAT genius to realize that if one state sends a 5% elite to compete against three-fourths of another state's student body, the elite will look good.

Will might or might not have known about the differences in rates across states. Bennett most assuredly did. It is depressing to see the author of *The Book of Virtues* being so cavalier about two of them, honesty and truth.

When a couple of researchers analyzed state-level SAT data taking into account the differences in participation rates, they found that the differences in participation rates accounted for 83% of the differences in SAT scores among the states. They also found that, when participation rates were taken into account, SAT scores rose by 15 points for every thousand dollars above the national average that a state spent on its schools.[17]

What about that other test, the ACT, from the American College Testing Program? Much of what has been said above about the SAT applies to the ACT as well. The ACT is another college admissions battery. It was developed in the 1950s by the American College Testing Program in Iowa. It differed from the SAT in that it tested more areas: reading, mathematics, science reading, and social

studies reading. Its items were more like those on achievement tests, although the SAT has now altered its items to bring them into closer alignment with the high school curriculum. The ACT also took more of a counseling and guidance focus in some of the background questions it asked students.

The ACT exhibited a decline similar to that of the SAT. Less attention has been paid to it for reasons of history, geography, and psychology. The SAT is a much older test, and it was developed in the East where more people live. But most important, the College Board and ETS have both been very energetic and successful in seeking attention from the media. The ACT people working out in Iowa have practically shunned media attention.

THE NATIONAL ASSESSMENT OF EDUCATIONAL PROGRESS (NAEP)

For many years NAEP was practically invisible. In 1994 I learned of someone writing her doctoral dissertation on the history of NAEP, a topic I was also working on at the time. I contacted her, and, in our ensuing correspondence, she apologized for being so enthusiastic about the topic. But, she said, "It is rare that have I the opportunity to talk to anyone who has even heard of NAEP." NAEP's low profile is not the result of bad tests or bad publicity. It is the legacy of a compromise that permitted NAEP to exist in the first place.

The idea for a national assessment occurred first to Francis Keppel while he was U.S. Commissioner of Education in the 1960s. (The Commissioner of Education was the highest federal education official when education was not a separate, Cabinet-level department, but part of the Department of Health, Education, and Welfare.) Keppel was impressed with how much the collection of health statistics had improved the health of Americans simply by calling attention to the rates of certain diseases. If you don't know how many cases of tuberculosis there are, it's hard to know how much of an effort you need to mount in order to eradicate it. Keppel didn't think the American education system was very healthy, and he wanted a means of demonstrating its pathologies to the public at large.

Keppel asked Ralph Tyler, an educator and at the time director of the Institute for Advanced Studies in the Behavioral Sciences at Stanford University, to undertake the project. Tyler, in turn, formed alliances with various testing agencies. We learned earlier that the goal of a norm-referenced test is to spread people out in order to make discriminations and differential predictions, while the goal of a criterion-referenced test is to hold performance up to some standard. Tyler had yet another notion of how to use a test. Tyler's idea for NAEP was simply to find out what is and what isn't — just as with health statistics. What do our kids know and what don't they know? To this end, Tyler thought NAEP should ask some questions that half of the students would know, as with a norm-referenced test. But it should also ask some questions that people felt almost everyone (90%) would know and some questions that virtually no one (10%) would be able to answer correctly. This would reveal what most people know, what some people know, and what most people don't know.

Tyler's logic went like this:

> The need for data on progress has been recognized in other spheres of American life. During the depression the lack of dependable information about the progress of the economy was a serious handicap in focusing efforts and in assessing their impact. Out of this need grew an index of production, Gross National Product, which has been of great value in guiding economic development. Correspondingly, the Consumer Price Index was developed as a useful measure of the changes in the cost of living and inflation. Education, today, is of great concern to all Americans. Without education our young people cannot get jobs, are unable to participate intelligently and responsibly in civic and social life, and fail to achieve individual self realization. Education is increasingly recognized as the servant of all our purposes.[18]

Therefore, Tyler argued, we need to know how well our servant is serving us. Keppel agreed with Tyler, although he was more interested in having our servant serve us better.

Before Keppel and Tyler got NAEP off the drawing boards, though, the very idea of NAEP was attacked by virtually every education organization in the nation and by a number of members of Congress as well. The National Education Association (NEA), the American Association of School Administrators (AASA), and the Association for Supervision and Curriculum Development (ASCD) all mounted blistering offensives directed at the concept. People argued that NAEP would stultify innovation, impede equal opportunity, bring pressure on administrators and teachers, and encourage cheating. Most of all, though, they opposed NAEP because they saw it as "the camel's nose under the tent," which would inevitably be followed by the whole camel, a federally written and controlled curriculum. To the education establishment of the day, a federal test would lead inexorably to a federal curriculum and so to the loss of local control. Local control of education then was an even more treasured aspect of public schools than it is today.

It is ironic that all the organizations that opposed NAEP's founding fully supported America 2000 and Goals 2000 — recent federal efforts to make national goals a national priority. It is still more ironic that groups on the religious and secular Right have opposed these recent federal efforts, in part, for the same reasons as the education groups had earlier opposed NAEP — an unwarranted imposition from the federal government (one book even describes Goals 2000 as part of a CIA mind-control plot).

In order to get NAEP off the ground, Tyler and his colleagues had to agree not to report state- or district-level results. NAEP would issue reports for the nation, for regions (e.g., the Northeast), for gender, for ethnicity, and for urban and rural areas. Except for tracking national trends, this made the data virtually useless to people at the state and local level.

From the beginning, NAEP attempted to devise novel forms of test items. Of course, some of the questions were multiple-choice, and some remain that way today, but open-ended questions are also employed. NAEP continues today to be a mixture of multiple-choice and open-ended items.

The original contract for NAEP was awarded to the Education Commission of the States (ECS), a policy-tracking body based in Denver, Colorado. ECS, as an organization sponsored by state governors, was seen as a safe place for NAEP, keeping it away from the influence of federal agencies. Initially, ECS was awarded the NAEP contract on a "sole source" basis — i.e., no other organization could compete for the contract. As NAEP expanded, pressure grew to award the relatively lucrative contract by competitive bid, the way most contracts are let. In 1982, as a result of just such a competition, the contract for NAEP passed from the Education Commission of the States to the Educational Testing Service, which began to seek publicity for NAEP by referring to it as "The Nation's Report Card."

In 1988, an amendment to the NAEP legislation permitted the reporting of state-level data, and about 40 of the states have participated in state-level assessments in reading, mathematics, and, starting in 1996, science. The rest of the states have abstained, mostly, they argue, because states must pay for the state-level results, and the information is not worth the cost.

NAEP still remains out of sight of most people because there is no feedback below the state level. Teachers never know how their charges did — nor do the students or their parents or anyone else. Although it has not been documented by research, many people feel that because NAEP has no significance to anyone's life, people don't take it seriously. When a district in which I worked in Colorado participated in a NAEP state-level field test, about half of the teachers involved reported to me that they had trouble keeping the students on task. It seems likely, therefore, that NAEP systematically underestimates the level of achievement displayed by American school children.[*]

[*] I offer this tentative conclusion because being motivated to do well on a test is no small matter. When I was director of testing for the state of Virginia, the tests had become so important to the public image of the schools that the districts were employing a significant number of what the state superintendent referred to as "inappropriate administrative procedures" — cheating to the rest of us.

We devised a computer program to detect unusual patterns of changes in test scores. One year, the computer spit out the name of a small, largely rural district, and in our role as policemen, we visited the superintendent to figure out what had happened. Although it was a rural area, the district was located near some suburban districts, and the same newspaper that covered the suburban schools also reported on this district's test scores. Typically, newspapers report test results in a "box score" format, list the grades tested the curriculum areas tested, and the percentile ranks attained in the curriculum areas at each grade. The inevitable comparisons were not favorable to the rural district.

The superintendent told us that most of the students in the district were not going to college, but would be going to work on their parents' farms or in farm-related industries. Most of them knew pretty much what they would be doing when they finished high school. The tests played no role in their future and, therefore, the superintendent said, "They don't take these tests seriously." To make students more serious about the tests, the superintendent decided to take them out of the academic arena. He presented the tests, not as an opportunity for the students to show how smart they were or how well their teachers had taught them, but as a chance to beat their archrivals in the adjacent county, just as they tried to do each year in football, basketball, and baseball.

And it was true that, if you asked a student in these schools what they were going to do with the tests, they would say "Beat — County!" (naming the archrival adjacent county). During the week of testing, the teachers dressed as cheerleaders and led pep rallies in the auditorium, where the students in the affected grades were cheered on by their nontested peers. In short, the motivational program worked. Depending on age and test topic, the scores that the computer found suspicious were 15 to 30 percentile ranks higher than the previous year's marks.

After the appearance of *A Nation at Risk* in 1983, the political appointees of the U.S. Department of Education began to seek a new use for NAEP scores. Whereas Tyler and his colleagues had seen NAEP only in descriptive terms, showing what students did and did not know, others — notably former Assistant Secretary of Education Chester E. Finn, Jr. — wished to use NAEP prescriptively: to show what students should know.

To this end, Finn, as the chairman of the National Assessment Governing Board (NAGB, pronounced NAG-bee) gathered groups of people together to rate the levels of the items and establish standards by which students would be placed at levels called "basic, proficient, and advanced." The first round of such standard setting produced a set of standards that indicated that virtually no students had skills that would permit them to cope with college-level material and indicated as well that many students did not have the skills to function at the grades in which they found themselves. Although NAGB wished to use the standards to sustain the sense of crisis that had been created by *A Nation at Risk,* the standards it set were so high that they seemed outlandish even to the ideologues at NAGB.

Another round of standard setting resulted in slightly lower but still exceptionally high standards. These standards had their problems, too. A team of well-known evaluators (hired by NAGB to evaluate both the standard-setting process and the standards themselves) pronounced the standards "technically indefensible." NAGB summarily fired the team. Or, at least, NAGB tried. The contract forbade such summary action. Other reviews of the standards by the Center for Research in Evaluation, Standards, and Student Testing; by the U.S. General Accounting Office; and by the National Academy of Education also found the standards problematical. The National Academy declared that the standards should come with a "warning label" pronouncing them "suggestive," not "definitive."

Still, politicians, ideologues, and some educators take the standards as given, and it is not hard to find people clucking over such "facts" as "Only

7$\frac{1}{2}$% of our three million high school seniors leave their secondary school experience with an ability to integrate scientific information with other knowledge." Even President Clinton has gotten into the act, declaring that "only 40% of our third-graders can read independently." This last "fact" is based on a rather loose interpretation of the NAEP levels, but it has served as the basis for his proposal for a national test in reading and mathematics.

This is an important point because it bears very much on how we feel about our schools. The children that the President says have trouble reading are the same children that finished second in the world in a comparison of third-graders from 27 countries. The survey agency, Public Agenda, has characterized the overall test performance of American students as "dismal." On the other hand, University of North Carolina psychometrician Lyle V. Jones recently said, "Efforts to fix cut scores in NAEP to separate achievement levels, Basic, Proficient and Advanced, have not been successful. Recent results from the Third International Mathematics and Science Study show that math performance for U.S. fourth-graders is significantly above the international average [for the 26 participating countries]. Yet, the NAEP report for 1996 shows only 18% of fourth-graders Proficient and only 2% Advanced in math. When U. S. 4th graders perform reasonably well in international comparisons, isn't it unreasonable that only 20% are reported to be Proficient or better?"[19] Given that these fourth graders were third in the world among 26 nations, I would certainly answer Jones' question with a hearty "Yes."

The principal problem with the NAEP levels is this: according to the NAEP procedures and the associated rhetoric, if a student tests at particular level in, say, mathematics, then we should be able to specify what kinds of math problems he will get right and what kinds he will get wrong. But it doesn't work out that way. The various studies mentioned above found that students at a particular level of mathematics get some items right that they ought not to be able to cope with and get some items wrong that they ought to be able to do easily.

A second problem with the NAEP levels is that words such as "advanced" lack any precise meaning, because they are not linked to anything else in the world. Consider, by contrast, the statement that "in order to have a 50-50 chance of passing college algebra, you have to score at X level on the ACT college admissions tests." This "level" on the ACT is linked to a real world event: passing college algebra. And it is linked to that real world event because the psychometricians at ACT followed 250,000 high school seniors through their college careers in order to see how students with different scores fared. From a score on the ACT tests, they can predict the likelihood that a student will earn a passing grade in college algebra (and, of course, in other college courses). This gives their levels an anchor in reality that is missing from NAEP.

Indeed, it is not possible to make this kind of linkage with NAEP. Because NAEP wants to ask a wide variety of questions and because it also doesn't want to intrude on a lot of class time, no student takes all of a NAEP test. All students take a certain portion, and the particular items that different students take are different. Of course, all items are given to enough students so that NAEP can estimate what proportion of students nationwide would get the item right. But no student ever has a score for the whole test.

Lacking a test score tied to a particular student, we cannot track any individual to see whether the "advanced-level" students do that much better than the students who were merely "proficient." Thus the levels have no firm connection to reality and are of questionable validity. It is a curiosity to me that so many people are willing to say astonishingly negative things about the NAEP levels in private but not in public.

To get the NAEP levels, we must rely on the judgment of panels whose members rate the items according to their difficulty. But these judgments are not linked to anything else that would allow us to establish their validity. Thus for one person the "advanced" level in mathematics might mean "able to go to college and pass college algebra," while for another it might mean "ready to go to college and take college calculus," and for yet another, "ready to take AP calculus in high school." These three judgments reflect vastly different levels of actual attainment. NAEP will be stuck with squishy levels and standards as long as there are no students taking an entire test. NAEP is currently undergoing a redesign, but it seems unlikely that the new design will incorporate so radical a change.

IQ Tests

No tests have caused more controversy than IQ tests, so it certainly behooves us to know something about them. IQ tests originated in France at the beginning of the 20th century, when the French Ministry of Education assigned a clinical psychologist, Alfred Binet, the task of constructing tests that would identify children who could not benefit from normal schooling. Binet, a kindly and humane sort, struggled with his assignment, knowing that his tests would have life-altering outcomes for some of the children who did poorly on them. Recall that tests as we know them did not exist then. Binet was essentially starting from scratch.

Among the things that Binet did was to ask teachers what kinds of tasks caused their students the most difficulty. And he developed at least some of his tests from such considerations. Thus it should not have surprised anyone that students who scored low on the tests would have difficulty in school, since teachers had already said that these tasks caused difficulties.

In the end, Binet concluded that the nature of the individual tests was not all that important. What was important was that there be a lot of them. In 1911 he wrote that "a particular test isolated from the rest is of little value; . . . that which gives a demonstrative force is a group of tests. . . . One test signifies nothing, let us emphatically repeat, but five or six tests signify something." Binet was developing a concept later referred to as "intelligence in general."

If a student did poorly on a given test, that wouldn't be so bad if she did better on another five or so tests. None of the tests held any more value for Binet than any of the others. If one student did well on tests 1, 2, 3, 4, and 5, but not 6, that outcome was the same for Binet as that of another student who did well on tests 1, 2, 3, 5, and 6, but not 4.

This equivalence for Binet was emphasized by a concept he developed and called "mental age." Binet decided that the tests would be of little use if children of different ages did not differ in perform-ance. They should do better as they got older, he reasoned. So Binet developed a system for classify-ing the tests according their mental age. A test was said to have a mental age of, say, 6 if 80% to 90% of the 6-year-olds could complete it successfully. That is, if 90% of 6-year-olds performed a particu-lar test successfully, while lower percentages of 4- and 5-year-olds and even higher percentages of 7- and 8-year-olds performed successfully, then that test was said to have a mental age of 6.

Binet also decided, somewhat arbitrarily, to have each of his tests count for six months of mental age. This was as far as Binet went with his scaling, placing the tests at various positions on his scale of mental age and summing the number of tests passed to obtain an individual child's mental age. The first scales appeared in 1905, with revisions in 1908 and 1911. The 1905 scale was "normed" on about 50 children already deemed normal, while the 1908 scale used some 300 such children; the 1911 scale was a minor revision. While Binet incorporated some tests that involved sensory and perceptual tasks, his scales emphasized verbal functioning, especially judgment, comprehension, and reasoning.

It was not long before a German psychologist, Wilhelm Stern, pointed out that by itself a mental age of, say, 8, was ambiguous. The meaning of a mental age of 8 would depend greatly on the chronological age of the person. A 5-year-old with a mental age of 8 would be quite advanced; a 12-year-old with the same mental age would be quite backward. Stern suggested that Binet divide the mental age by the chronological age and multiply by 100 to get rid of the decimals. For a 5-year-old, this means 8/5, yielding a quotient of 1.6, which, multiplied by 100, yields 160. For a 12-year-old, this means 8/12, yielding a quotient of .67, which, multiplied by 100, yields 67. Stern suggested that this quotient be called the Intelligence Quotient or IQ.

Later on, other psychometricians pointed out that the intelligence quotient, as a genuine quotient, had troublesome statistical properties of its own. A child of 5 with a mental age of 8 would get an IQ of 160. A child of 10 with a mental age of 13 would get an IQ of 130. Yet, in terms of mental age, both chil-dren would be three years ahead of their chrono-logical age. This problem was "solved" by going to what is called the "deviation IQ." At all age levels, raw scores are converted into standard scores with a mean of 100 and a standard deviation of 15 (see page 58 and pages 33-34 for a discussion of stan-dard deviations and standard scores respectively).

A child who has the median score for his chrono-logical age gets an IQ of 100. A child who is one standard deviation above the mean gets an IQ of 115 (the standard deviation having been set arbitrarily at 15). And so forth.

When Binet's notion of "intelligence in general" crossed the Atlantic, it underwent a curious trans-formation and became "general intelligence." Binet had warned that many tests were necessary to capture the complexity of "intelligence in general." But the notion of "general intelligence" seemed to suggest a more singular, unitary concept that affected all aspects of life.

The idea that intelligence might be a single entity dovetailed nicely with the rediscovery of Mendelian genetics, which seemed to suggest that very complex traits could be controlled by a single gene. Thus three ideas caused a great deal of excitement in the early testing community in the U.S.: 1) intelligence influences every aspect of life, 2) intelligence is a unitary entity controlled by a single gene, and 3) IQ tests measure intelligence.

To these early psychometricians — Robert Yerkes, Carl Campbell Brigham, H. H. Goddard, and Lewis Terman (who had developed Binet's scales into something he called the Stanford-Binet IQ Test) — these three ideas opened up the possibility of a nearly ideal society, a society in which the rewards that society offered would be justly distributed to those who were most deserving — namely, those who were the most intelligent.

Aside from the fact that the ideas are all are eminently challengeable, the big problem with the early testing movement was that the psychometricians involved were both hereditarians and racists. They also believed, with the strength of religious conviction, that they were right. Indeed, they *knew* they were right. I stress this point because, even today, psychometricians are influenced by this legacy and sometimes act more like members of a religious order than members of a disinterested scientific society.

Although it was Yerkes who invented the multiple-choice format that permitted the mass testing of groups and although it was Terman who developed the famous Stanford-Binet test, it was Goddard who was the most politically active, influential, and enthusiastic of the early testers. In the early 1920s, he would go down from his office at Columbia University to meet the boats at Ellis Island and administer IQ tests to immigrants. He had no compunction about declaring that at least three-fourths of those landing at the time — largely Poles, Czechs, Hungarians, Italians, Greeks, Slavs, and Eastern European Jews — were mentally unfit.

It apparently never occurred to Goddard that many of these new arrivals had never attended school or had never held a pencil in their hands until he thrust one at them. He never questioned the translators' ability to create a valid test in another language on the spot. Nevertheless, Goddard prevailed in promulgating his conclusion that the new arrivals, many from Eastern and Southern Europe, were not nearly as bright as the Northern European immigrants who had preceded them. He convinced Congress to roll back the immigration quotas to the 1890 numbers that were much more favorable to those from the nations of Northern Europe. In 1924 President Coolidge signed the legislation saying, "After all, America must be kept safe for Americans." Goddard and the others also thought that American society had already done a pretty good job of sorting people out by ability. "The people who are doing drudgery are, as a rule, in their proper places," he said.[20] He told an audience of Princeton freshmen:

> Now the fact is, that workmen may have a 10 year intelligence while you have a 20. To demand for him such a home as you enjoy is as absurd as it would be to insist that every laborer should receive a graduate fellowship. How can there be such a thing as social equality with this wide range of mental capacity?

Elsewhere, Goddard made it clear how the new social order was to be created. "Democracy means that the people rule by selecting the wisest, most intelligent to tell them what to do to be happy. Thus Democracy is a method for arriving at a truly benevolent aristocracy."

This was hardly a new idea in American society. Thomas Jefferson had proposed a program of education for the state of Virginia that would sort out each year the best minds and allow them to continue their education at state expense. (Those who could afford it could send their children of whatever talent to school for as long as they liked.) By this means, Jefferson thought we would arrive at an "aristocracy of worth and genius," in contrast to the European aristocracy that was solely determined by the accident of birth. Jefferson, though, held that intelligence was equally distributed among rich and poor classes. Goddard would have said that Jefferson labored under a terrible delusion.

Against the psychometricians' arguments that IQ was determined by genes — nature — there arose another school of psychologists who claimed that intelligence was strongly affected by the environment — nurture. The nature/nurture controversy has seesawed back and forth ever since the earliest claims of the psychometricians. And it continues today. At times it seems to favor genes; at other times, the environment.

In 1995 *The Bell Curve* made a forceful — but not entirely sound — argument in favor of nature. A recent study, much touted by both President and Mrs. Clinton, indicates the importance of infantile stimulation in the development of connections in the brain, a finding strongly in favor of nurture. As an either/or proposition, the nature/nurture debate is silly. And false. Obviously, both are important. Part of the reason the evident silliness of the debate has remained obscure is that those on different sides of the argument have cited different kinds of research evidence to support their claims. Naturists use correlational research; nurturists use experimental data.

To see the difference this makes, consider the following hypothetical experiment. Let us assume, for the sake of argument, that we have six sets of parents. Both parents in each pair have the same tested IQ (again we'll ignore the possibility of "measurement error"). Let us give each set of parents a set of identical twins. The genetic makeup of such twins is identical; thus their "nature" is identical. Each set of parents gets to raise one twin, and we assume that the parents will act in ways that will tend to make the child have an IQ similar to theirs. The other twin is raised by other parents coached by psychologists and educators who provide the kind of intellectual, cognitive stimulation that seems likely to increase IQ; thus the nurture of the second twin is quite different from that of the first. At the end of six years (about as early as a child's IQ becomes stable enough to rely on), we measure the IQ of our sets of twins. The results are shown below.

	Parent IQ	Twin 1 IQ	Twin 2 IQ
Parents 1	100	100	150
Parents 2	101	101	151
Parents 3	102	102	152
Parents 4	103	103	153
Parents 5	104	104	154
Parents 6	105	105	155

The statistic known as the correlation coefficient (discussed on pages 63-65) measures the relationship between two variables, in this case, the relationship between the parents' IQ and children's IQ.

In the case of the parents and Twin 1, the correlation is perfect because as the IQs of the parents rise, so do those of the children and in a perfectly predictable way. The two sets of IQs are perfectly correlated. The value of the correlation coefficient is +1.0. Thus we would be inclined to say that genes played a big role in the determination of the IQs of the children known as Twin 1 because the correlation between parents' and children's IQs is so high.

What about Twin 2? The correlation between parents' IQs and the IQs of those called Twin 2 is also a perfect +1.0. To get a perfect correlation, the two numbers do not have to be identical. All that has to happen is that as one number (e.g., parent IQ) increases, the other number (child's IQ), increases in a perfectly predictable way. The measured IQ of each Twin 2 is irrelevant to the correlation coefficient. Recall that the correlation coefficient measures only the relationship between two variables. Looking at parents' IQs and at the IQs of the Twin 2s, we see that, as the parents' IQs increase,

so do those of the children and in a perfectly predictable way. Once again, genes loom large.

But the IQ of each Twin 2 is, in each case, *50 points higher* than that of the parents or of Twin 1. This makes it appear that the intellectual stimulation provided by the researchers — i.e., nurture — had a huge impact. An IQ of 100 is at the 50th percentile; an IQ of 150 is above the 99th percentile.

The body of literature concerning the relative influences of nature and nurture shows that correlational research always makes genes seem important, while experimental research highlights the impact of nurture — although the effects are not nearly as large as in our hypothetical study. Correlational research, naturally, uses correlation coefficients. Experimental research reports data in terms of mean differences induced by the experimental treatment. In this case, our experimental treatment induced a mean difference of 50 IQ points between parents and Twin 2s.

There is another aspect of the nature/nurture controversy that is conceptually flawed. The controversy assumes that all "parts" of intelligence are equal. Thus it has been common for naturists to claim that IQ is 80% inherited and 20% determined by the environment. But it could well be that the 20% affected by nurture is the most important 20%, the 20% that makes us distinctly human. As far as I know, the hereditarians have never considered this possibility.

There are a variety of tests that yield a measure called IQ. Perhaps the most famous are the Stanford-Binet and the Wechsler. The Wechsler was initially constructed by psychologist David Wechsler at Bellevue Hospital in New York City and called the Wechsler-Bellevue. Later, two separate IQ tests were developed from the first version, the Wechsler Adult Intelligence Scale, WAIS (pronounced, wayis), and the Wechsler Intelligence Scale for Children, WISC-R, (pronounced, wisc are) the "R" standing for "revised" after the test was revised in 1974.

The Wechsler was developed in part in reaction to the Stanford-Binet's emphasis on verbal skills. The Wechsler gave equal attention to "performance" tests such as completing pictures, arranging pictures, copying geometrical designs with a set of blocks, putting objects together, and solving mazes. In later years, the areas covered by the two tests have converged. For instance, the WISC-R contains a verbal scale as well as a performance scale, consisting of vocabulary, arithmetic, comprehension, the judgment of similarities, and the processing of verbal information.

Other tests in this general category include the Otis-Lennon School Ability Tests, the Woodcock-Johnson, and the Peabody Picture Vocabulary Test. The last has the advantage of being relatively fast to administer individually. Some IQ tests have also been developed to administer in group settings. The correlations among these various tests are typically quite high.

Is IQ "unitary"? As discussed above, those who developed IQ tests operated on the assumption that it reflected a unitary mental process, usually referred to a g for general. This unitary process affected virtually everything a person did. It did not take long for another school to develop contending that there was no g factor, that intelligence was made up of a series of separate, independent abilities.

Howard Gardner, a cognitive psychologist at Harvard University, has recently put a spin on this part of the intelligence discussion that has received considerable attention in educational circles. In 1983 Gardner published *Frames of Mind,* in which he argued that to reduce human abilities to a single number as in IQ was misleading — and wrong. Gardner posited seven intelligences: verbal-linguistic, logico-mathematical, spatial, bodily-kinesthetic, musical, intrapersonal, and interpersonal. All people possess all seven intelligences to some degree. Skills in verbal and logico-mathematical are typically what is measured by IQ tests and what schools emphasize (recall that Clinton's national test is in reading and math).

Spatial intelligence is associated with artists or architects. Bodily-kinesthetic intelligence is demonstrated by dancers and athletes, musical by the various musical performers. A person high in intrapersonal intelligence is a person who can "get in touch with himself." People high in interpersonal intelligence can read other people well.

Other people have noticed talents such as musical talent, of course, but have relegated it to a sphere outside of "intelligence." They have argued, like Goddard, that intelligence is a unitary trait that influences virtually all behavior. Gardner by contrast, elevates these talents to the same level as traditional IQ and chides schools for being so dominated by verbal-linguistic and logico-mathematical intelligence.

CHAPTER 7

Getting Technical

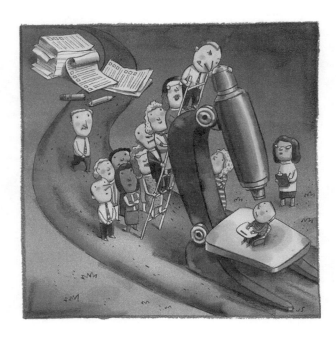

letter sigma "Σ" while each value is represented by an *x*. The symbol for the mean is sometimes capital M, but more often a capital X with a horizontal bar over the top and called "X bar" ($\overline{X}$). In the distribution of "scores" listed below the sum of all 11 numbers is 35,000,460,000. This sum, divided by 11, yields a mean of 3,181,860,000.

FIGURE 3 Distribution of Wealth	1. 10,000
	2. 10,000
	3. 20,000
	4. 25,000
	5. 45,000
	6. 50,000
	7. 55,000
	8. 75,000
	9. 80,000
	10. 90,000
	11. 35,000,000,000

$$\Sigma \chi = 35,000,460,000$$

$$M \text{ or } \overline{X} = \Sigma \chi/n = 35,000,460,000/11 = 3,181,860,000$$

S ooner or later, if you deal with test scores, you will encounter a number of terms that have precise technical meanings. This chapter defines and discusses those terms.

Measures of Central Tendency. The terms mean, median, and mode all refer to some kind of average or, as statisticians say, a measure of central tendency.

The *mean* is what most people think of as an "average." We all learned to calculate a mean in school. You just add up all the numbers and then divide by the number of numbers. The symbol for "to add up all of the numbers" or "to sum" is represented in statistics by the capital Greek

The use of one value — 35 billion — so much larger than the rest is not an accident. That figure is the estimated wealth in dollars of Bill Gates, founder of Microsoft, in August 1997. The other values are arbitrary and represent the wealth of other residents of Microsoft's home town, Redmond, Washington. For convenience, we have populated Redmond with only 10 people other than Gates.

These 11 values were chosen to illustrate an important fact: the mean is affected by extreme values. And if such extremes are extreme enough or occur with some frequency, they will lessen the degree to which the mean fairly represents an average — that is, a central tendency. In the case shown above, the "average" wealth is over three billion dollars, while, in reality, only one resident has wealth that high, and none of the rest have wealth even as much as one ten-thousandth as high.

One way of describing an average where extreme values have no impact is the *median* (usually written as Mdn). By definition, half of all scores are above the median, and half are below. We have been using one median throughout this book — the 50th percentile of a distribution of test scores. The national norm of a test score distribution is a median. In the distribution in Figure 3, half of the scores fall above $50,000, and half fall below that figure so the median is $50,000. Since we are just counting how many people score above a point and how many people score below it, Bill Gates is just another guy — for our purposes, equal to everyone else. For the data presented in Figure 3, the median is a "better" average in that it better represents the wealth of the residents of our simplified version of Redmond.

The final way of representing an average is called the *mode*. It is simply the score that occurs most commonly. In Figure 3, the mode is 10,000, even though that value is also the lowest score in the whole distribution. Again, an average might not be a meaningful representation of the group.

> The media translated average into "mediocre" — although the first is a statistic and the second a judgment that might or might not be accurate.

Now, if a distribution is "normal," that is, if it the scores form a bell curve, then all three measures of average will be identical.

If they are not identical, that is one way you have of telling that the distribution of scores is not a normal distribution without looking at the actual distribution. This feat (knowing whether or not scores are distributed normally) is not particularly important for teachers except for this: many of the calculations used by statisticians concerning test scores presume a normal curve.

If the scores are not distributed normally, a number of calculations lose their validity, most notably the test for statistical significance, which we'll discuss shortly. In many cases it would probably be wise to make a graph of the distribution of scores to get a visual impression of how much it deviates from a bell curve. Whatever term is used for average, it is often misinterpreted. In the Third International Mathematics and Science Study (TIMSS), for instance, American eighth-graders got 53% of the items right while the international average was 55%; in science the American kids got 58% correct while the international average was 56%. We thus finished very close to average in both subjects.

The media translated average into "mediocre" — although the first is a statistic and the second a judgment that might or might not be accurate.

What the media failed to note was that most countries got very similar scores. The 58% correct in science put America in 19th place among the 41 countries in the study. Bulgarian students managed to get 4% more correct. This sent them soaring to fifth place. Icelandic students got 6% fewer items correct. This sent them plummeting to 30th place. Note that the difference between Bulgaria and Iceland is only 10%, but this makes a difference of 25 ranks (Bulgaria 5th, Iceland 30th). Thus, if America is "mediocre," the world is mediocre. Of the industrialized nations of Europe and Asia, only Finland and Taiwan did not participate in TIMSS.

Measures of Dispersion. A law everyone learns in elementary statistics — and then immediately forgets — is "no measure of central tendency without a measure of dispersion." Means, medians, and modes — measures of central tendency — should never be used in isolation, although they usually are. And they can be misleading as this old joke about three statisticians shows. Three statisticians went deer hunting. They had not been out long when they spied a huge 12-point buck. The first statistician fired and missed by exactly 10 inches to the left. The second statistician then fired and missed by exactly 10 inches to the right. The third statistician exclaimed, "We got him!"

Measures of dispersion give some idea of how the scores are distributed around the average. The simplest measure of dispersion is the *range*. If the children in your class all score between the 23rd percentile and the 92nd percentile on a test, then the range is 69 percentile ranks (92 minus 23), or we would simply say that the range is from 23 to 92.

Although it is always good to know the range of scores, the range might not be particularly useful because, like the mean, it can be affected by extreme scores. For the data in Figure 3, the range is enormous, even though most scores are tightly bunched around a much lower value. In fact, a single extreme score has more impact on the range than on the mean. Gates' wealth alone defines one end of the range, but it is only one of 11 values that go into calculating the mean.

The most common measure of dispersion is called the *standard deviation*. I give the formula for those who want to know how it is calculated. Anyone else can skip this part.

$$SD = \sqrt{\frac{\Sigma (X - \overline{X})^2}{N}}$$

The important thing about the standard deviation is its relationship to the normal curve. We know, for instance, that in a normal curve, 34% of the scores lie between the mean and one standard deviation below the mean. Another 34% lie between the mean and one standard deviation above it. Between one and two standard deviations in either direction lie roughly another 14% of the scores. The standard deviation is used in the calculation of standard scores, as discussed on pages 33-34. It is also used in the calculation of statistical significance and effect sizes, which we take up in the following section. If you want a visual impression of the standard deviation, look back at the normal curve shown on page 32. The vertical lines inside the curve depict the location of standard deviations from -3 on the far left to +3 on the far right.

Statistical Significance and Effect Size. I give the concept of statistical significance special treatment for two reasons: 1) it is the most technical concept in the booklet, and 2) it is a very important concept that is often misinterpreted.

A result that is statistically significant is often interpreted as if that result were practically significant. In fact, you cannot make any judgment about practical significance from statistical significance, and that is the main reason that I have made statistical significance share this section with its less famous sidekick, effect size. To begin to make judgments of practical significance, you need to know an effect size (or something like it).

It is particularly important not to confuse statistical significance with educational importance. I recommend that you supplement the material you read here with a two-part series by James Shaver, "Chance and Nonsense: Conversations About Interpreting Tests of Statistical Significance," which appeared in the September and October 1985 issues of the *Phi Delta Kappan*. Shaver presents the material in an easy-to-read format as a conversation between two teachers in the teachers' lounge.

Tests of statistical significance are usually performed in experiments involving two or more groups. Let's take the simplest case of just two groups. Figure 4 below shows the results of an experiment, let's say, teaching one group of first-graders to read using a whole-language approach and teaching another group using a phonics approach. At the end of the year of teaching, the children were given a reading test (let's assume that the test is equally fair to both approaches in terms of what it tests). Two normal curves are generated, one each for the scores of the children taught by the two methods. The difference between the two groups is represented by the letter D or, sometimes, the Greek letter Δ (delta).

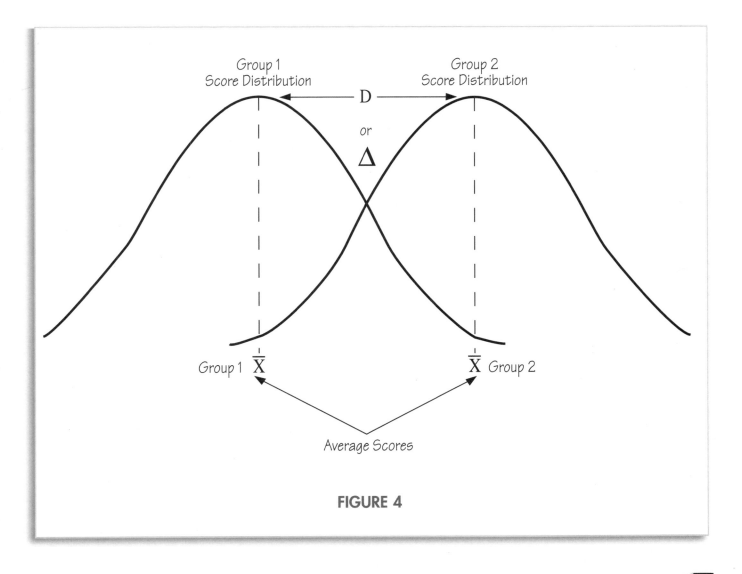

FIGURE 4

As educational practitioners, we want to know whether phonics or whole language is the better method of teaching reading. The traditional approach to answering this question is through a test of statistical significance. But statistical significance tells you nothing about the impact of a treatment, even though people almost always act as it if does.

Now, here comes the most technical concept in this treatise. You found that the two groups differed by some amount. You do some statistical calculations to see if the results are statistically significant. Here is what the test for statistical significance tells you: *How likely is it that you would find a difference (D or Δ) between the two groups as large as you did find if the two groups really did not differ? Or, as the statisticians say, if the two samples came from populations with the same mean.*

The keys to the paragraph above are the words "How likely." A statement of statistical significance is a statement of likelihood, of odds, of probability. It is *not* a statement of magnitude. "How likely" is the result you found due to real differences? How likely is it that these differences occurred by chance? A statement about statistical significance is *not* a statement about the magnitude of those differences. On matters of magnitude, statistical significance is silent.

The point bears repeating. Statistical significance speaks to odds. What were the odds of finding the results you did find if there really is no difference between the groups? If the odds are small enough, the result is said to be statistically significant. Typically, results are considered significant if the statistical test for significance says that your result would happen by chance less than five times in 100. I don't think this is an adequate criterion, although most researchers use it. Personally, I don't want to try to build a discipline on results where I can be wrong one time in 20. I prefer the next level of significance usually reported where the odds of the result happening by chance are one in 100.

When researchers talk about statistical significance, they say things like "*p* less than point oh five" or "*p* less than point oh one." The first is their way of describing the first level of significance given in the paragraph above — one chance in 20 that the results are due to chance. The second describes the more stringent level — one chance in 100 that the results are due to chance. When they write it down, the statements of significance look like this: $p < .05$ and $p < .01$. (The letter *p* stands for probability of seeing the observed results by chance, and < is the mathematical symbol for "less than.")

A "*p* less than point oh one (.01)" does not mean, to go back to our example, that whole language had more impact on beginning reading than if we found a "*p* less than point oh five (.05)." The *p* stands for a probability. If you get a $p < .01$, you're not very likely to be wrong if you say there's a real difference between whole language and phonics.

If you're not familiar with statistical significance testing, you can be forgiven for wondering what all the fuss is about. You gave the tests, the two groups differed, what's the problem? Why do we even need these tests?

The problem is that you didn't test everyone or, as statisticians say, the entire population. If you gave the test to all first-graders in the country, you wouldn't have to conduct a test of significance (we'll ignore the issue of "measurement error" here and assume for the sake of this argument that our tests are perfect measures). Whatever differences you found would be real, and that would be the end of it.

But no one can afford to test all 3,000,000 or so first-graders in the U.S. So we perform our experiments on small numbers of students — on samples. And usually we use what researchers call samples of convenience: we test the kids in the local schools. Any time you take a sample of a population, there's a chance that your sample is not representative of the whole population. This introduces the possibility that if you *did* test the whole population, your results would be different than the results with your samples.

The samples used in educational research are often quite small, perhaps only two classrooms, so the possibility that they are not representative of the nation as a whole is substantial. The chance that we have nonrepresentative samples in our experiments is increased by the fact that most of our samples are not random samples. To have a random sample all 3,000,000 first-graders in the country would have to have an equal chance of being chosen for the experiment. But, again, such a procedure for most research would be prohibitively expensive and impractical. You'd have to go all over the country testing kids or bring kids from all over the country to a central location. Not readily done, so most researchers use samples of convenience: the kids they can find the neighborhood schools. The only regular testing conducted in this country that uses genuine random samples is the testing carried out by NAEP. *

The fact that we use samples of convenience brings up an important and often ignored aspect of educational and psychological research: studies need to be replicated. Replication is the norm in the natural sciences, but not in the behavioral sciences. When two guys in Utah claimed they had accomplished cold fusion, a process that would revolutionize energy use and bankrupt the OPEC nations (you wouldn't need oil), laboratories all over the world swung into action to see if they could reproduce the results. In the natural sciences, a fact is not a fact until lots of people have demonstrated it is so. But, for some reason, replication has never had this honorable status in the behavioral sciences.

The use of an "effect size" (ES) is an attempt to transform results from statements of probability into a quantitative form that addresses, well, effect size. To take the simplest case of two groups again, suppose we instruct one group with a program designed to increase problem-solving ability and a second group, the control group, receives no such treatment. At the end of the treatment, we give a problem-solving test to both groups.

*The notion of error introduced by sampling is not really a new notion to most people, although they might not recognize it in this context. Any time you see a Gallup or Roper or Harris poll reported, you will see a footnote that the poll has a "margin of error" of plus or minus 4% (or 3% or 5%, etc.). What this means is, "We sampled a certain number of people in our poll, and we got the results we show you. If we sample another group, the results might not be precisely the same, and this 'margin of error' gives you an estimate of how different the results could be."

Pollsters could use random samples if they wished since they are dealing with adults by telephone and only a tiny minority of people do not have a phone in the home. But they don't use random samples because they want to guarantee that their samples have certain demographic characteristics. Pollsters have extremely sophisticated ways of sampling and can make statements about national results with samples of only about 1300 well-chosen people. Educational research, alas, is not in a position to conduct such research. We are usually stuck with samples of convenience — the kids nearby.

A test of statistical significance will tell us how likely we were to see whatever differences we find if the two groups really didn't differ. The calculation of the effect size will tell us how much impact the training had, if it had any at all. To calculate an effect size, we simply subtract the mean of the control group from the mean of the experimental group and divide by the standard deviation of the control group. Here are some made up data to provide an example:

Example 1

Control Group: $\overline{X} = 50$, SD $= 10$

Experimental Group: $\overline{X} = 60$, SD $= 12$

$$ES = \frac{60 - 50}{10} = \frac{10}{10} = +1.0$$

Example 2

Control Group: $\overline{X} = 73$, SD $= 12$

Experimental Group: $\overline{X} = 70$, SD $= 14$

$$ES = \frac{70 - 73}{12} = \frac{-3}{12} = -.25$$

TABLE

What do we have here? We have one version of a standard score, which is discussed on pages 33 to 34. You might want to jump back and reread those pages before proceeding. The difference between an effect size and the standard scores described earlier is that the standard scores are for individuals, and effect sizes are for groups. For the sake of argument, let's say we get an effect size of +1. What does that mean? It means that the average score of the students who received the training in problem solving was as good as the 84th percentile of the kids in the control group. Recall that a standard score of +1 is a score one standard deviation above the mean. Fifty percent of all scores are below the mean, and another 34% are between the mean and +1 standard deviations, hence a total of 84% (we could also say that the size of the effect is equivalent of taking a child at the 16th percentile and moving him to the 50th, or taking a child at the 84th percentile and moving him to the 98th; each of these moves is a distance of one standard deviation).

And that means the treatment was very, very powerful. A treatment that moves a child from being average to being well above average is not often seen. We don't usually get effect sizes of +1 or larger. So judging how big an effect is big enough to be of practical significance is a point somewhat debated among researchers. Some think that an effect size begins to take on practical importance when it's about +.25. Others are more conservative and hold out for +.35. If you get an effect size of +.3, this is equivalent to moving a person who initially scored at the 50th percentile out to the 62nd percentile. (This is something that you could know only by looking it up in a table in a statistics book.)

To take a more real-life example, African American students score about one standard deviation below white students on a variety of tests. An educational treatment that produced an effect size of .33 for African American students would wipe out the ethnic difference in only three years.

An effect size is not the ultimate answer to our questions about practicality. Suppose your new curriculum in problem solving cost you $7,000, as a one time investment. An effect size of +.3 for this money would be one thing. Suppose, though, that the new curriculum cost $7,000 a year. Or that it cost $70,000. Would it still be a worthy investment? There is no quantitative way of making this decision. The program and its benefits must be weighed against other potential uses for the money.

Effect sizes have another important use, although this one is more often limited to the research community. Although replication is not often done, numerous researchers do work in the same general areas like mastery learning, computer-assisted instruction, etc. Their research studies don't match each other completely, and summarizing the research in a given area was difficult until effect sizes were developed. We can take the entire body of research on a given topic and convert all the outcomes into effect sizes. When we do that, we can average the effect sizes to see what the whole body of research says as a single number. For instance, one study looked at the average effect size of all the research on retaining kids in a grade for a second year. After calculating effect sizes from hundreds of studies, the researcher found that the average effect size for all the research was -.15. Retention in grade harms children. If it helped, the effect size would have been positive.

Why all this fuss over statistical significance and effect sizes? The average reader doesn't conduct experiments. But more and more, school districts and intermediate units and states do. And so, too, does the nation. The results from the Third International Mathematics and Science Study (TIMSS) were released showing the 41 countries in the study in three groups: those that were significantly above the U.S., those that were significantly below, and those that did not differ significantly from the U.S. score. The *Orange County Register* in California looked at these three groups and reported that American students finished in the next-to-last group. Of course, such a "finish" is

inevitable unless American students had scored so high that no country was significantly higher, or so low that no country was significantly lower.

Districts, states, and nations increasingly present their findings in terms of statistical significance and effect size. Without some knowledge of these terms, you cannot decide whether the results are being properly presented. I have attended a number of school board meetings where results from testing or research were presented as statistically significant with no explanation of what this term means.

The Correlation Coefficient. Sooner or later, mostly sooner, anyone dealing with tests is going to come in contact with correlation coefficients. When the SAT is used to predict freshman grade-point averages, the statistic used to make that prediction is the correlation coefficient. If your student takes a "spatial relations test" and the high school counselor mentions that people who score high tend to make good pilots, someone, somewhere, has correlated the test with success in flight school. When we examine the relationship between parents' IQ scores and those of their children, the statistic used is the correlation coefficient.

There are a variety of correlation coefficients, but the one most often used is officially known as the Pearson Product-Moment Correlation Coefficient. It correlates scores or the numbers assigned to any two variables (e.g., SAT scores and college freshman grade-point averages). Another coefficient sometimes seen is the Rank-Order Correlation Coefficient. It correlates ranks and is an approximation of the Product-Moment correlation coefficient. If you were interested, for example, in the relationship between nations' ranks on economic competitiveness and ranks on the eighth-grade mathematics scores from the Third International Mathematics and Science Study, you would use the rank-order statistic. (Incidentally, the correlation in this case is +.09, meaning there is virtually no correlation.)

Both correlation coefficients can take on values ranging from +1 to -1. A correlation of +1 means that there is a perfect correlation between the two variables: as one gets higher, the other gets higher in a perfectly predictable way. A correlation of -1 also means that there is a perfect correlation between the two variables, but now, as one variable moves higher, the other moves lower in a perfectly predictable way. A correlation of 0.0 means that there is no correlation: given a high score on one variable, we can't make any prediction about the value of the other variable. It might be high, average, or low.

When graphed, perfect correlations are straight lines, and a zero correlation is a circle. For values in between, the graphs of correlations are ellipses. Figure 5 shows perfect correlations, zero correlation, and two correlations in between, one strong and one weak.

The graphs of correlation coefficients are called "scatter plots" and it is usually a good idea to look at them. The correlation coefficient assumes that the relationship between the two variables is linear. But it might not be. Looking at the scatter plot will tell you whether or not the linearity assumption has been met. If it has not, the correlation coefficient will not provide a good test of the strength of the relationship. The last example in Figure 5 shows a strong, but non-linear relationship between two variables. The correlation coefficient would underestimate the true strength of this relationship.

In the section on statistical significance, we presented an example in which we tested to see if two groups in an experiment differed significantly. Significance tests can be applied to correlation coefficients also. Here the significance test determines the odds of your obtaining a correlation

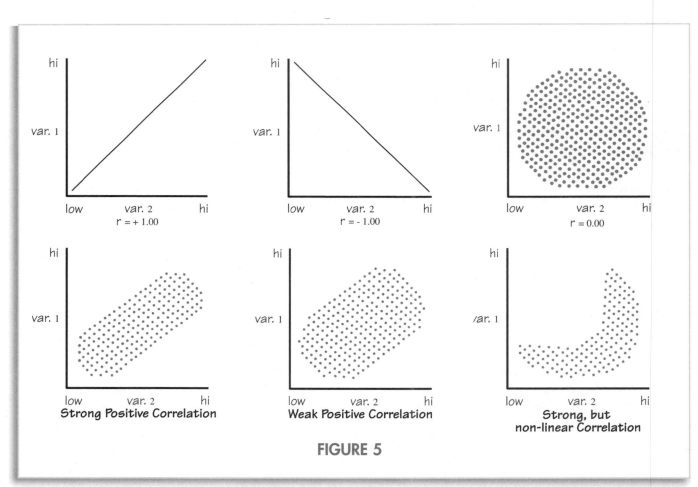

FIGURE 5

as large as the one you did get if the real correlation between the two variables is zero.

There are times when I consider forming the National Association for the Abolition of Correlation Coefficients because they cause so much misunderstanding. The reason is this: *correlation says nothing about causation.* Everyone who has even a passing acquaintance with statistics knows this. But human beings have an apparently irresistible impulse to infer causation from correlation. Given a correlation between variable A and B, it might be that variation in A causes variation in B. It might equally be that variation in B causes variation in A. Or it might be that variation in A and variation in B are actually caused by some third variable C. Or there might not be any causal relationship between A and B at all. For example, there is a strong correlation between arm length and the length of one's shirt sleeves. But, given nothing but the correlation coefficient, it makes as much sense to say that increasing the length of sleeves will increase the length of one's arms as to say the reverse.[*]

Remember this: any two variables can be correlated. That doesn't necessarily mean that the resulting correlation coefficient is meaningful. There is a correlation between which conference wins the Super Bowl and which political party wins the presidency. Before everyone started wearing jeans, there was a correlation between hemlines and prosperity: short hemlines meant good times; long ones indicated recessions. No one, so far as I know, proposed during a recession that we shorten skirts to cure our economic woes. From correlation, you cannot infer causality (but the temptation to do so seems to be hard-wired into our brains.)

Reliability. The essential question to ask of a test is, is it valid? A prior question, though, is to ask, is it reliable? Validity is addressed in the next section.

A reliable test is one that gives the same results each time (taking into account measurement error, also discussed below). A test that gives a different score each time a person takes it is not a reliable test (although, because of measurement error,

> There are times when I consider forming the National Association for the Abolition of Correlation Coefficients because they cause so much misunderstanding. The reason is this: correlation says nothing about causation.

[*] In early 1998 the U. S. Department of Education enshrined a causal inference from a correlation that had earlier been noticed by the College Board: children who take algebra as eighth or ninth graders tend to take rigorous courses of study and are much more likely to go to college than children who do not take algebra at all or who take it in a later grade. Another way of phrasing this finding is to say that there is a correlation between taking algebra and going to college. The Board and the Department are now pushing an algebra-for-everyone crusade on the assumption that if more kids take algebra early, more will go to college. It is just as likely, though (more likely in my opinion), that the students who take algebra early are those whom the school has already identified as college material. Requiring all children to take algebra might result in the discovery of a few kids the school had misidentified, but it also could result in turning a lot of kids off to school.

Something like this might be happening in Milwaukee which imposed algebra on all ninth-graders in the school year 1993-94. Previously, only 36% of Milwaukee ninth-graders took algebra and 60% of them passed. The current pass rate is 53% . One can wonder whether the algebra course that 53% of all kids pass has the same level of rigor as the earlier course that of 36% of the students passed. Moreover, a failure rate of 47% means that over *three thousand* Milwaukee students fail each year. What happens to them? Are they put off school? More likely to drop out? Unfortunately, Milwaukee doesn't have the data to demonstrate what happens. Other indicators of achievement such as the proportion planning to attend four-year colleges, though, do not show the kinds of improvements that the algebra-for-all folks would predict.

test-takers seldom get *precisely* the same test scores). The extent to which a test is reliable is assessed by looking at the reliability coefficient which is nothing more or less than a correlation coefficient or the estimate of a correlation coefficient.

There are several coefficients available. The best, and one that is almost never calculated, is the correlation between the test taken at time 1 and the same test taken again at time 2. This kind of reliability coefficient is called a test's test-retest reliability. Time 2 should be picked so that memory from time 1 doesn't influence the outcome and so that the events happening between Time 1 and Time 2 don't influence the results at Time 2. Time 2 used to be given in textbooks as several weeks, but since no one calculates test-retest reliabilities anymore, it is not clear that this is still thought of as a standard. Indeed, as one test textbook notes, there really is no such thing as *the* test-retest coefficient because the reliability decreases with increasing time between tests.

Money is the main reason no one does test-retest reliabilities. Time is also a factor. It takes twice as much of each for test-retest reliability as it does for all other reliability coefficients which come from a single test-taking session.

Something that comes close to test-retest reliability in terms of truly establishing reliability is alternative form reliability. Most testing companies develop two forms of their achievement tests that can be used interchangeably.

Another reliability coefficient is the split-half correlation. In this case, half of the test is correlated with the other half, sometimes first half with second half, but more often odd-numbered items with even-numbered ones. Of course, if you have a 50-item test and correlate odd- and even-numbered items, this is the same as correlating

two 25-item tests, and the result is a reliability coefficient for only a 25-item test. There is a statistical procedure for finding out what the reliability coefficient is for the entire 50-item test.

Finally, the most common correlations today are variants on the split-half correlation. The two most common of these are called the Kuder-Richardson-20 (usually abbreviated to KR-20) and Cronbach's Alpha. These are based on the proportions of people passing and failing each item. The KR-20 is, mathematically, the average of all possible split-half reliabilities. This fact has some practical significance. The KR-20 should be used only when one is certain that all of the items in a test are measuring a single dimension.

To see why this is so, imagine a test with 10 vocabulary items, 10 spatial relationship items, 10 arithmetic reasoning items, and 10 perceptual speed items, in that order. In doing a split-half reliability coefficient among odd and even items, you would be correlating scores on only one dimension: the five odd vocabulary items with the five even vocabulary items, the five odd spatial items with the five even and so forth. In a KR-20, though, which calculates all possible split-halfs, in some of these calculations, a person's scores on vocabulary items would be correlated with her scores scores on arithmetic items and so forth. Since people differ in their relative performance on these four skills, the reliability coefficient would be reduced.

Validity. Once a test is known to be reliable, it can be checked for validity. There are various kinds of validity, too. We'll take a peek at only four, content validity, criterion validity, curriculum validity, and instructional validity.

Content validity simply asks the question, "Does this test measure what it claims to measure?" In the matter of school subject areas, this is not often a major issue. In some other arenas, though, the test questions come at the topic of their test somewhat obliquely. Even in school matters, though, a test can lack content validity. If a test of mathematics that used nothing but set theory were imposed on students who had learned mathematics in some other way, we wouldn't think that the test was a good measure of their achievements.

Criterion validity is another correlation coefficient, one calculated between performance on the test and performance on some criterion. In the case of the SAT, for instance, the criterion is freshman college grade-point average. The SAT is supposed to predict grades, and, if it doesn't, it doesn't have criterion validity.

A test is said to have curriculum validity if the content measured by the test is present in the curriculum used by the school. It has instructional validity if the content of the test is actually taught. These concepts grew out of a court case in which a test qualifying students for high school graduation was challenged on the grounds that some children had not had any opportunity to learn what the test was covering. The courts ruled that the state could use the test, but only after some years in which the state had to establish that the material on the test had actually been taught. It is worth mentioning in passing that the judges on the case used the phrase, curriculum validity, but when one reads their brief, one sees quickly that they are in fact talking about instructional validity.

Since this case, in the late 1970s, the organizations sponsoring test standards have adopted the court's major finding: that those using school-related tests to make important decisions about students must show that the students have had a chance to learn the material covered by the test. Many state testing agencies have developed a code of ethics for test use which also calls for test users to insure such validity.

I said earlier that a test must be reliable before it can be valid. There are some areas of performance assessment, however, where some would argue, me included, that validity is possible in the absence of reliability. To cite an actual case: I once submitted an article to a journal that then sent the article to four reviewers who assessed its adequacy for the journal. The review form had four categories: "publish as is," "publish with minor changes," "publish with major changes," and "reject."

The four judges used all four categories, each picking a different one. At one level, one would say that the "test" is unreliable since the judges couldn't agree and that we should scrap the peer review process of deciding what gets into our professional journals. Some people actually claim this. Reading the judgments, though, it was clear to me that that they gave the paper different ratings because they held different perspectives on what was being said (reviews are done anonymously and so can be shared with authors without jeopardizing relations between reviewers and writers). Each judgment was valid from its perspective.

These kinds of differences occur in many complex human endeavors. For instance, in one city I lived in that had two newspapers, I sometimes wondered if the papers' two movie critics had actually seen the same film, so divergent were their observations and opinions.

These kinds of differences, although not so severe, show up in some school assessments as when different teachers give different grades to the same portfolio or oral presentation. What is important is to have some person to make an informed, final decision. In the case of my papers, an editor who could review all the reviews; in the case of the critics, the moviegoers or would-be moviegoers make their own assessment of the reviewers; in the case of portfolios, some teacher who can act as the editor did.

The Standard Error of Measurement. This is a technical term we will deal with only in conceptual terms, not bothering with the formula. It would be nice if tests were perfectly accurate, but they aren't. There is some amount of error associated with them, and it is called measurement error. The usual statistical procedure for calculating the amount of error is to compute the standard error of measurement, a straightforward procedure using other statistics concerning the test. The standard error of measurement is a variety of standard deviation.

The importance of the standard error of measurement is this: if it is large, important decisions using the test's results probably shouldn't be made. The test isn't accurate enough. Suppose we have a test score for a person. That is called, simply enough, the observed score. In theory, the observed score might or might not be what is called the true score. We can then use the standard error of measurement to ask, "Given this observed score and this standard error of measurement, what is the range of scores within which we can be pretty certain the true score lies?" For instance, given an observed score of 70 and a standard error of 2, we can be pretty certain that the person's true score is between 66 and 74 (plus or minus two standard errors).

Measurement error can have large practical ramifications. In the court case mentioned earlier, a school district wanted to retain children who did not score at a particular level. However, the standard error of measurement of the test was large enough that a child who scored one point below the passing score for third grade could actually have a true score that would be above the passing score not only for third grade but for fourth, fifth, and sixth!

In another instance, when a passing score was set for the National Teacher's Examination, a specific cut score or passing score was first determined. Given the fact that there is some measurement error on the NTE, as on all tests, the passing score was then moved one standard error below the original cut score. This meant that most, although not all, test-takers who had true scores above the passing score would not fail the test just because of measurement error.

CHAPTER 8

Conclusion

To end this book, consider the following editorial about testing from the September 25, 1997, issue of the Ft. Wayne Indiana *News Sentinel*. It is neither particularly good nor particularly awful. It is rather the kind of material you are likely to encounter in the nation's media.

Read the editorial and write your reactions on a separate piece of paper. If you wish, you can compare your comments to mine, which appear on pages 70-71. (The numbers in the editorial refer to my comments.)

ANALYZE OBJECTIONS TO GRADUATION TESTS

Sometimes the best justification for something is provided by the arguments against it. That's certainly the case with Indiana's new ISTEP-Plus test, which students must pass in order to graduate from high school.(1)

Among the chief objections to the test is the very real possibility that thousands of Hoosier teens will be unable to pass it, causing considerable anxiety for students and considerable embarrassment for those who have failed to educate them.(2)

If that sounds like proof of the test's necessity — and it should — 'you ain't heard nothin' yet'.

This test is administered in the sophomore year. Students who fail are given four more chances to pass it, and may be able to graduate even if they never pass the test by maintaining a "C" or better average in their core work.(3) Surely an educational system worthy of the name should be able to teach students to pass a test given in the 10th grade by the time they are in the 12th grade.(4)

But even that seemingly simple task is misleading. The tests in question actually are based on ninth-grade academic standards.(5) In other words, the angst surrounding this test stems from the fear that many Indiana seniors are incapable of doing freshman-level work.(6)

Nor is that fear unjustified. If the requirement had kicked in the last year, 45 percent of sophomores statewide would have been placed at risk of not graduating by failing one or both of the test's math and English portions.(7) The failure rate would have been higher at many urban school districts.

It is true that tests by themselves neither teach nor improve the skills of those who do. But the educational process clearly does require some objective way of determining what has been learned — otherwise, there is no way of knowing when to end one lesson and begin another.

Effective teaching demands that problems be exposed and corrected — not ignored or excused.(8) As a diagnostic tool, there simply is no substitute for standardized tests. Grades and teacher evaluations have their place, but do so objective standards. They provide a hedge against grade inflation and allow a meaningful comparison of schools across district and state lines.(9)

Reprinted with permission
The Ft. Wayne *News Sentinel*

My Comments:

1. The first question that comes to my mind is, "Is it a good idea to have a test that students *must* pass in order to graduate?" The various teacher assessments of the students in the form of grades come from a much more extended observation of the student. Was this test *designed* as a graduation hurdle or was it designed for another purpose and just appropriated for this new one? The Testing Standards adopted jointly by the American Educational Research Association, the American Psychological Association, and the National Council for Measurement in Education strongly oppose using a test designed for one purpose for another purpose. In this case, the original purpose of the test could be critically important: a larger standard error of measurement can be tolerated for a test used at the building or district level than for one used to make judgments about individuals.

In addition, should the incentives used to promote learning be negative? "Pass this test or else" appears to be what the state is saying to the students.

2. Will this test really be an indication that teachers "have failed to educate" students who cannot pass the test? Students, after all, are not blank slates or passive blobs of clay. Some will actively resist what the teacher tries to teach them. Discussion about factors that contribute to test results appear on pages 13-14. Incidentally, Indiana students score about the national average in the National Assessment of Educational Progress' assessments of reading and mathematics.

3. The fact that the test is administered in the sophomore year is some consolation. If students have five chances to pass a test, they are much less likely to fail by chance. But will the test be in the same form all five times? Or are there various other forms floating around? If the latter, what kind of equating study was conducted to ensure that all of the forms are parallel?

The word "may" in the passage "may be able to graduate" is ambiguous. I take it to mean that students with "C" averages don't have to pass the test, but it could mean that students with "C" averages and failing test scores will be reconsidered and that they have *some* possibility of graduating, but also *some* possibility of *not* graduating.

4. Does this focus on teaching kids to pass a test mean that other parts of the curriculum will be neglected? (Remember the law of WYTIWYG).

5. What does the phrase "ninth-grade academic standards" mean? Does it refer to some kind of "grade level?" If so, we have to keep in mind that "grade level" usually means the point above which and below which half the students score. Nationally, half of our high school

diplomas are awarded to people who score below the 12th-grade level. By definition, "grade level" does not have to be defined this way, but is almost always is.

6. If the seniors are incapable of doing freshman-level work, does that constitute a crisis? It is not clear. But the statement clearly implies that the editorial writers have in their heads the notion that the level of achievement advances by a fixed amount each year in high school. The reality is obviously much more complex. Clearly, seniors read better than freshmen (as reflected in NAEP reading scores for eighth- and 12th-graders), but many people argue that a ninth-grade reading level is sufficient for most reading tasks in the real world. Some students take no more math after the freshman year. One might expect these students to do worse as seniors than they would have at the end of their freshman year. Does this mean that instructional time will have to be taken from other areas to refresh these students' math skills? Is this the best use of such time?

7. Does a test that 45% of the sophomores fail say more about the sophomores or the test? Without further information it is impossible to tell. Again, if the test is truly "ninth-grade level," the sophomores might be about where one would expect them. The 45% represents students who failed reading *or* math as well as those who scored low on both.

8. The final paragraph falls into the trap of thinking that tests are "objective measures." Yes, they are not subject to teachers' judgments. But are teachers' judgments mere "subject-ivity" or do they represent nuanced judgments that a test cannot make. Moreover, while tests are "objective" in that all students take them under the same conditions, someone — some "subject"— decided what was going to be on the tests in the first place. As noted in the text, though, teachers tendencies towards higher grades, real or simply perceived, have increased the trust people place in test scores.

9. "They… allow a meaningful comparison of schools across district and state lines." In a pig's eye! We have noted elsewhere that test scores are highly subject to the influence of family and community variables. We know well in advance of any test that affluent communities will outperform poor communities. This by itself is in no way a "meaningful comparison across district lines." It could well be that a poor district is doing more with the available resources than an affluent community which could be "coasting" on the knowledge that its students are likely to do well in any event. For cross-district comparisons to be meaningful, the context variables of the communities, such as poverty rates and parental educational levels, have to be taken into account.

It is to be hoped that by the time you reach this point in the book, you have some better idea of how tests are made, what they can and can't do, and how to interpret the results from them. The technicalities of tests have been covered in brief. Anyone interested in pursuing them further might wish to peruse Lee Cronbach's *Essentials of Psychological Testing* (Harper & Row) or Anne Anastasi's *Psychological Testing* (Macmillan).

It is not likely that we will reduce our reliance on tests any time soon. Although the President's proposal for a national test has met, at best, a lukewarm reception in the statehouses around the country, it is not because the governors are anti-test. For the most part, they are pushing their own test development programs and simply think that such programs are better operated at the state rather than the national level. The best we can hope for is that you can use the knowledge gained from this book to keep tests in their proper perspective.

Notes

1. Roughly half, anyway. It depends on whether the college is using a "mean" or a "median" as its definition of "average." Highly selective colleges are more likely to use a mean; open enrollment colleges are more likely to use a median. All of this is explained in more detail in later sections.

2. Grant Wiggins, *Assessing Student Performance*: *Exploring the Purpose and Limits of Testing* (San Francisco: Jossey-Bass Publishers, 1993), p. 72.

3. F. Allan Hanson, *Testing Testing: Social Consequences of the Examined Life* (Berkeley: University of California Press, 1993), p. 179.

4. Desmond Hanerd, "The Failed Miracle," *Time*, 22 April 1996, p. 60.

5. Mary Jordan, "School Bell Takes Its Toll in South Korea," *Washington Post*, 7 May 1996, p. 1.

6. "Reforming Japan's Schools," *Principal*, January 1998, pp. 24-27.

7. Alexandra K. Wigdor and Wendell R. Garner, eds., *Ability Testing: Uses, Consequences, and Controversies, Part II* (Washington, D.C.: National Academy Press, 1982), p. 317.

8. Anne Anastasi, *Psychological Testing*, 6th ed. (New York: Macmillan, 1988), p. 414.

9. Lee J. Cronbach, *Essentials of Psychological Testing,* 4th ed. (New York: Harper & Row, 1984).

10. Jason Millman, "Criterion-Referenced Testing 30 Years Later: Promise Broken, Promise Kept," *Educational Measurement, Issues, and Practices*, Winter 1994, p. 19.

11. Lauren B. Resnick, *Education and Learning to Think* (Washington D.C.: National Academy Press, 1987), p. 3.

12. Daniel P. Resnick and Lauren B. Resnick, "The Nature of Literacy: An Historical Explanation," *Harvard Educational Review*, vol 47, 1997, pp. 370-85.

13. Dave Barry "The ABCs of the SATs," *Washington Post Sunday Magazine*, 12 October 1997.

14. Wilford M. Aikin, *The Story of the Eight-Year Study* (New York: Harper and Brothers, 1942).

15. William H. Angoff and Henry S. Byer, "The Admissions Testing Program," in William H. Angoff, ed., *The College Board Admissions Testing Program* (New York: College Entrance Examination Board, 1971), pp.1-13.

16. Gerald W. Bracey, "SAT Scores: Miserable or Miraculous?" *Education Week*, 21 November 1990, p. 36.

17. Brian Powell and Lala Carr Steelman, "Bewitched, Bothered, and Bewildering: The Use and Misuse of State SAT and ACT Scores," *Harvard Educational Review*, Spring 1996, pp. 27-59.

18. Ralph Tyler, "Assessing the Progress of Education," *Phi Delta Kappan*, September 1965, p. 14.

19. Lyle V. Jones, "National Tests and Education Reform: Are They Compatible?" Speech delivered at Educational Testing Service, Princeton, N.J., May, 1997. Available at http: //www.ets.org/research/pic/jones.html.

20. This Goddard quote and those that follow are taken from Stephen Jay Gould's scholarly yet eminently readable book *The Mismeasure of Man* (New York: Dutton, 1981). I highly recommend it to readers interested in the history of the measurement of intelligence.